Exploring and Applying the Parables

The Parables of Jesus found only in the Gospels of Matthew and Mark

John Belham

PARVA PRESS

Copyright © 2025 by John Belham

The right of the author has been asserted.
All rights reserved. No part of this publication may be reproduced, distributed or transmitted in any form or by any means, without prior written permission.

Parva Press
Web: https://www.parables.org.uk
E-mail: parvapress@parables.org.uk

Principal Scripture quotations are from the ESV* Bible (The Holy Bible, English Standard Version*) copyright © 2001 by Crossway, a publishing ministry of Good News Publishers. Used by permission. All rights reserved.

Supporting references marked RSV and some allusions are drawn from the Revised Standard Version of the Bible, Copyright 1952 (2nd edition 1971) by the Division of Christian Education of the National Council of the Churches of Christ in the United States of America. Used by Permission. All rights reserved.

Book Layout © 2017 BookDesignTemplates.com
Cover design and layout SJB

British Library Cataloguing in Publication Data.
A catalogue record for this publication is available from the British Library.

ISBN 978-0-9537489-5-2

To the glory of God
and the stirring, strengthening
and encouraging of his people

"He who has ears to hear, let him hear."

"Enter by the narrow gate. For the gate is wide and the way is easy that leads to destruction, and those who enter it are many. For the gate is narrow and the way is hard that leads to life, and those who find it are few."

CONTENTS

Introduction 1
   Alphabetical list of the parables explored 3
The Sower 5
The Growing Seed 19
The Weeds Sown Among the Corn 31
The Hidden Treasure and the Pearl of Great Value 45
The Net of Fish 55
New and Old Treasures 63
The Lost Sheep 71
The Unmerciful Servant 85
The Vineyard Workers 97
The Two Sons 113
The Wedding Feast 127
The Wise and the Foolish Virgins 141
The Talents 151
The Sheep and the Goats 163
Final Words 175
Principal Sources 177
About the Cover Images, the Author and his Other Publications 181

Introduction

Sinclair Ferguson comments that, even today, the parables continue to challenge our human thinking in society and in the church. They meet us where we are – and then either challenge us or encourage us.

Having written on the parables of Jesus found in the Gospel of Luke, the aim in this second volume is to explore, in the order in which they are recorded, a number of the well-known parables found only in the gospels of Matthew and Mark, exploring each parable in its original setting, and then seeking to apply its teaching to our current situation in the world of today.

The book is not intended to be an academic text, but a book for group or personal consideration.

The Lord scattered parables and memorable pictures large and small throughout his teaching. Sometimes his vivid word pictures were in clusters of two or three, yet together forming a single portion of his teaching, and so it is often helpful to explore them together.

This selection of parables is offered with the prayer that it might be used of God for the challenging, stirring and building up of his people.

Questions for personal reflection or discussion
The questions at the end of each parable are offered: Firstly, to help us to see and take hold of the promises our Lord gave. Secondly, to help us to recognise his warnings – and to heed them.

Acknowledgement
The author gratefully acknowledges his debt to the many godly commentators who, over the centuries, have mined the treasures of these parables. He acknowledges his eternal debt of gratitude to the One who first told them.

Approach

Writing in the 1800s, Richard Trench, Dean of Westminster and then Archbishop of Dublin, commented that each parable is like '. . . a casket, itself of exquisite workmanship, but in which jewels yet richer than itself are laid up . . .'

I tremble to handle the words of my Lord, but prayerfully aim to look within:

- To take note of the occasion that gave rise to the Lord telling the parable, and the particular people to whom it was addressed.
- To note the way our Lord himself interpreted and applied it, and the way it was understood by the apostles, who profited from the teaching and put it into practice in their lives.
- To avoid interpretations that, although the parable might be understood in that way at a much later date, including our own, were clearly not intended to be understood that way by his hearers at the time the parable was told.
- To avoid reading into the parables the kind of 'creative' interpretations our over-active imaginations can so easily supply!

Alphabetical list of the parables explored

The Growing seed – 19
The Hidden Treasure and the Pearl of Great Value – 45
The Lost Sheep – 71
The Net of Fish – 55
The New and Old Treasures – 63
The Sheep and the Goats – 163
The Sower – 5
The Talents – 151
The Two Sons – 113
The Unmerciful Servant – 85
The Vineyard Workers – 97
The Wedding Feast – 127
The Weeds Sown among the Corn – 31
The Wise and the Foolish Virgins – 141

The Sower

That same day Jesus went out of the house and sat beside the sea. And great crowds gathered about him, so that he got into a boat and sat down. And the whole crowd stood on the beach. And he told them many things in parables, saying: "A sower went out to sow. And as he sowed, some seeds fell along the path, and the birds came and devoured them. Other seeds fell on rocky ground, where they did not have much soil, and immediately they sprang up, since they had no depth of soil, but when the sun rose they were scorched. And since they had no root, they withered away. Other seeds fell among thorns, and the thorns grew up and choked them. Other seeds fell on good soil and produced grain, some a hundredfold, some sixty, some thirty. He who has ears, let him hear."

Then the disciples came and said to him, "Why do you speak to them in parables?" And he answered them, "To you has been given to know the secrets of the kingdom of heaven, but to them it has not been given. For to the one who has, more will be given, and he will have an abundance, but from the one who has not, even what he has will be taken away. This is why I speak to them in parables. Because seeing they do not see, and hearing they do not hear, nor do they understand. Indeed, in their case the prophecy of Isaiah is fulfilled that says:

'You will indeed hear but never understand, and you will indeed see but never perceive. For this people's heart has grown dull, and with their ears they can barely hear, and their eyes they have closed, lest they should see with their eyes and hear with their ears and understand with their heart and turn, and I would heal them.'

But blessed are your eyes, for they see, and your ears, for they hear. Truly, I say to you, many prophets and righteous people longed to see what you see, and did not see it, and to hear what you hear, and did not hear it.

Hear then the parable of the sower. When anyone hears the word of the kingdom and does not understand it, the evil one comes and snatches away what has been sown in his heart. This is what was sown along the path. As for what was sown on rocky ground, this is the one who hears the word and immediately receives it with joy, yet he has no root in himself, but endures for a while, and when tribulation or persecution arises on account of the word, immediately he falls away. As for what was sown among thorns, this is the one who hears the word, but the cares of the world and the deceitfulness of riches choke the word, and it proves unfruitful. As for what was sown on good soil, this is the one who hears the word and understands it. He indeed bears fruit and yields, in one case a hundredfold, in another sixty, and in another thirty."

Matthew 13:1-23 English Standard Version

The Sower – a key to the parables

Introduction to the parables
Jesus used a great many parables as he taught and challenged the different groups among his hearers.

Jesus taught the great crowds in parables to capture and hold their attention, and to open the ears of 'those with ears to hear' to the nature of the kingdom of heaven. As he taught them, he also warned them of some of the difficulties they would face if they seriously wanted to enter the kingdom of heaven, and be part of it.

The religious leaders were always in attendance and often challenged Jesus by their questions and by their attitude. By parables, Jesus showed them, as in a mirror, what they were doing by holding so fast to their traditions. By doing so, they were blinding themselves to the words of the prophets and to what the Lord God was actually doing before their eyes in fulfilment of those prophecies.

Later in his ministry, through a series of parables, Jesus showed the religious leaders the consequences of their rejection of him. By hardening their hearts against the witness of John the Baptist, against himself and his teaching, and ultimately against God and his word by the prophets, they would bring about their own destruction.

Privately, to his own disciples and to others close to him whose eyes had been opened, he taught both directly and in parables. The parables found in Matthew chapter 13 are in two groups. Matthew records that Jesus taught the parables of the sower, the weeds in the field, the mustard seed and the leaven to the great crowds from the boat. The explanation of the weeds in the field and the parables of the discovered treasure, the precious pearl, the fish in the net and the well-trained scribe, were shared with the disciples more privately in the house, as they asked him about the parables.

'He who has ears, let him hear'
It takes 'opened eyes' and 'unstopped ears' to really hear and understand the spiritual battles that take place in the life of the true believer.

As John Bunyan wrote *Pilgrim's Progress,* he caused his pilgrim, Christian, to stay for a few days in the Interpreter's house. There the pilgrim was shown what was really going on hidden behind some of the great temptations, pitfalls and battles he would face on his journey.

The Lord Jesus was doing very much the same as he told the parable of the sower. This is why it is such a key parable. Many of the subsequent parables follow this pattern. Jesus was warning and preparing his hearers, and particularly his disciples, about the enemy's ploys, and the pressures the world will put on those who believe. Unprepared frail human beings can give up or give in, and so are prevented from truly hearing and understanding, and holding on to, the word of God and being fruitful before him.

The scenes Jesus describes can be sudden, or they may be so subtle and gradual that, completely unawares, they catch those who have not been warned, or who are failing to take his words seriously, and who are failing to walk warily and 'watch and pray'.

The disciples' question
Privately, in the house, the disciples – together with 'those who were around him,' as Mark records – asked Jesus, "Why do you speak to them in parables?" And Jesus said, "This is why I speak to them in parables. 'Because seeing they do not see, and hearing they do not hear …' The Lord's parables sifted and separated those really longed to know about the kingdom of heaven, from those who were hearing him and yet had no concern or interest in spiritual things or being forgiven and put right with the Lord God. They had no desire, as the Lord had promised through his prophet Isaiah, to 'understand with their heart and turn, and I would heal them.'

Jesus then went on to speak of himself to those whose eyes had been opened, "But blessed are your eyes, for they see, and your ears, for they hear. Truly, I say to you, many prophets and righteous people longed to see what you see, and did not see it, and to hear what you hear, and did not hear it."

The prophets spoke with longing, of the promised day when the Lord God would himself be the shepherd of his people, of the day when God would visit and redeem his people, of the day when Emmanuel, the anointed One, the Messiah, would come.

Simeon and Anna were watching and waiting, and they recognised the young child Jesus for who he truly was – God's promised One, Israel's glory and redeemer.

The long-promised Messiah was now among them, healing the sick, giving sight to the blind and hearing to the deaf, setting the spiritually bound free and causing the lame to leap with joy. He had compassion on the great crowds of poor and neglected people as he taught them by parables. These were the marks and signs of the arrival or 'advent' of the true Messiah spoken of by Isaiah.

However, it took and still takes spiritually opened eyes and unstopped ears, like those of Simeon and Anna, to hunger after the fulfilment of God's promises for the healing, the salvation and consolation, of God's chosen ones, and to see and realise who the Lord Jesus truly is.

A closer look at the Parable of the Sower
After Jesus had explained why he taught in parables, Matthew gives us a compressed account of Jesus' explanation of the parable of the sower. It is clear from the setting and the equivalent passages in the other Gospels that the seed is the word of God, or the word of the kingdom, and the soil is human hearts. The reception of the word depends on the condition of the mind and heart of the hearer.

The seed falling along the pathway
'A sower went out to sow. And as he sowed, some seeds fell along the path, and the birds came and devoured them.'

'When anyone hears the word of the kingdom and does not understand it, the evil one comes and snatches away what has been sown in his heart. This is what was sown along the path.'

'. . . their eyes they have closed, lest they should see with their eyes and hear with their ears and understand with their heart and turn, and I would heal them.'

Jesus plainly warned his hearers that we have an adversary who is eager to snatch away any possible benefit we might have gained from hearing the word.

Richard Trench comments, 'Man so opens and fills his mind with this world's thinking that it becomes as hard as a paved road, so that he has no ability to understand the things of eternity, all that speaks of sin, of redemption, of holiness, is unintelligible to him and without significance.' And there is 'one watching to take advantage of that evil condition, to use every weapon that man puts into his hands, against man's salvation...'

The scribes and Pharisees of Jesus' day had drawn their own conclusions concerning Jesus. For this reason their ears and eyes were firmly closed both to his teaching and to the evidence of who he truly was. Their hearts were as hardened as any well-trodden pathway.

For many others in the crowd, their hearts were less hardened, they just did not think about or take to heart the things they saw and heard. Jesus' 'stories' were a delight and they loved to hear them. But it never dawned on them that there might be any significance in the things he was teaching. They never took them to heart, and never really understood them. As soon as they returned home they forgot them and just got on with everyday life. Satan snatched the seed of the kingdom away.

For many years, I confess to being like so many of Jesus hearers. I must have heard hundreds of talks and sermons, but it never occurred to me to think that the words I was hearing might have any bearing on the way I was actually living. I simply had no ears to hear and so gave Satan every opportunity to snatch away what had been sown. It had yet to be 'given to me' to hunger after the 'secrets of the kingdom of heaven.'

Seed falling on rocky ground

'Other seeds fell on rocky ground, where they did not have much soil, and immediately they sprang up, since they had no depth of soil, but when the sun rose they were scorched.'

'As for what was sown on rocky ground, this is the one who hears the word and immediately receives it with joy, yet he has no root in himself, but endures for a while, and when tribulation or persecution arises on account of the word, immediately he falls away.'

The disciples took the trouble to ask the Lord why he taught in parables, and were hungry to know the meaning of the parables he taught. They asked him to explain them. But the crowds of people in general took no such interest and so didn't take any further steps to understand Jesus' teaching, they just enjoyed hearing him and seeing his miracles of healing.

The Scriptures consistently warn us that there will be times of difficulty, times of 'tribulation,' times when our faith will be sorely tested by our circumstances, or perhaps by other people.

In early teenage years, a little spark of faith had been fanned into flame as I was encouraged to read the Gospels and began to grow in spiritual understanding. However, as a family we moved to a new area, and so began many years without any spiritual encouragement. Without nourishment, the challenges and difficulties that might have strengthened deep rooted faith only caused the little, shallow rooted, faith I had to falter.

That is only one young man's experience. What of the great knocks and challenges of life? The shattering blow of family breakdown, or serious illness. The slow and painful process of coming to terms with the death of a loved one. The shock of being made redundant and perhaps being without a job for months. These things are so hard to bear, and in such times, if faith is to stand, it needs to be firmly rooted in a close walk with the Lord God and a sure grounding in his word.

Seed falling among thorns
'Other seeds fell among thorns, and the thorns grew up and choked them.'

'As for what was sown among thorns, this is the one who hears the word, but the cares of the world and the deceitfulness of riches choke the word, and it proves unfruitful.'

The cares of this world – Apart from the scribes and Pharisees and the tax gatherers, most of the people in the crowds listening to Jesus would have been very poor; scraping a meagre existence from what they could grow and sell, or trade with, or, like the disciples, earn from fishing. There was very little to spare, especially with the heavy tax burden laid on them by their Roman conquerors. So they were very open to the pressing anxieties, 'What shall we eat?' and, 'With what shall we be clothed?'

At present, in the comfortable and relatively wealthy West, most of us know almost nothing of such extreme hardship. However, there still has to be food on the table and a roof over our head, perhaps a family to support and certainly bills to pay. The times in which we live are also uncertain and employment very far from stable and secure. The stress and uncertainties of the modern world and work place, give us plenty of scope for the anxious cares of this world to all but consume us.

In a busy home with youngsters to attend to and perhaps elderly parents to help, there are already too many things to fit into each day. How easy it is, in such a situation, for godly time and opportunities for serving the Lord to be squeezed out. 'How I wish for more time for prayer, but the children must be taken to school.' 'How I wish for uninterrupted Bible study, but I've only got five minutes before I must be out of the house for work.' 'It would be so good to have more freedom to spend time with other Christian believers, but on returning home I'm so tired, and the evenings are taken up with settling the children down for the night.' 'How I wish to grow in faith and better serve my Lord, but...'

These things so easily creep up on us all but unnoticed until they all but stifle faith and fruitfulness before God.

The deceitfulness of riches – The cares of feeding a family by subsistence farming or fishing, when under Roman occupation and heavy taxation, were very great. The pleasures and allurements offered when the Romans smiled on you, as for example they did on the Pharisees, the Sadducees and the tax collectors, were compelling.

Wealth has about it an almost magnetic attraction. Many of us desire it. Some of us spend our lives pursuing it and some of us let the pursuit of it consume our entire lives. But as the Lord said, riches can be deceitful. Wealth promises so much; freedom to go where we want, do what we want, buy anything we want. However, wealth has a nasty habit of not delivering on its promises. As the prodigal son of our Lord's parable found, as he faced famine in a foreign land, because of the chances and changes of this life, wealth sometimes cheats us of the happiness and contentment we assumed it would bring.

Indeed, very far from wealth being our servant enabling us to live a fulfilled and purposeful life, in our pursuit of it and in our maintaining of it, we can become all but its slaves.

The religious leaders of Jesus' day were trapped in this way. The relative wealth and social privileges they enjoyed bound them. They could not afford to recognise Jesus as the promised Messiah. To do so would mean the loss of all the privileges they enjoyed as respected religious leaders. The cost of recognising Jesus as God's true Messiah was too great.

Can we too bind ourselves by wealth, position or our other interests? I love this beautiful planet on which we are set, and being of a scientific turn of mind would happily have spent all my time attempting to uncover some of its plant and medical secrets. Yet each of these pursuits, good and fascinating as they are, would have taken first place and hindered me from obeying the Lord God's primary call on my life. Like the seed falling among the weeds, it would have been choked.

Seed falling on good soil
'Other seeds fell on good soil and produced grain, some a hundredfold, some sixty, some thirty.'

'As for what was sown on good soil, this is the one who hears the word and understands it. He indeed bears fruit and yields, in one case a hundredfold, in another sixty, and in another thirty.'

'. . . this is the one who hears the word and understands it.'

The Lord deals with us as rational people and sows his word in our minds. The disciples had been given ears and minds to recognise that there was far more to Jesus' words, and given a hunger to understand them better. Unlike the main body of Jesus' hearers, the disciples wanted to know more, and asked Jesus to explain the parable. Jesus said to them, 'To you has been given to know the secrets of the kingdom of heaven, but to them it has not been given. For to the one who has, more will be given, and he will have an abundance, but from the one who has not, even what he has will be taken away.'

There are many levels to 'hearing and understanding the word.' Our understanding can be very superficial, very shallow, or it may grow to be very deep and life-changing.

An example would be the prayer Jesus taught his disciples; the prayer we often call the Lord's Prayer. A great many Christian folk know it well. We can recite it alone or together in a traditional or a modern form. We 'know' it. And yet we may have very little depth to that understanding. We know it by heart, but our hearts and lives are quite untouched by it.

As we come to understand the words of the Lord's Prayer with our hearts as well as our memories, it will constantly remind us to live seeking the honour of our heavenly Father, the extending of his kingdom and doing those things that please him – his will. The prayer will also teach us to walk with a grateful heart, acknowledging our utter dependence on the Lord's provision, guiding and protection.

Slowly growing to maturity on good ground
This same increasing depth of understanding applies to all of our Lord's teaching – his parables, his direct instruction as well as his pattern of life, as he constantly lived to do his Father's will. Under the hand of God, may the Holy Spirit stir us to hunger, not just to know

the teaching of our Lord superficially, but to 'understand with our hearts'.

To gain such 'understanding with our hearts' requires time. For the disciples, it was time set aside to spend with the Lord, listening to him and asking him questions. For us it means time with his word, prayerfully meditating on it – as the psalmist puts it, 'hiding the word in our hearts.' It is not instant. Nor do the fruits of such growth in spiritual understanding come to maturity immediately. Perhaps that is why Luke's account of the parable of the sower concludes with, 'As for [the seed] in the good soil, they are those who, hearing the word, hold it fast in an honest and good heart, and bear fruit with patience.'

A varied range of fruitfulness
'Other seeds fell on good soil and produced grain, some a hundredfold, some sixty, some thirty.'

'As for what was sown on good soil, this is the one who hears the word and understands it. He indeed bears fruit and yields, in one case a hundredfold, in another sixty, and in another thirty.'

The Lord God blesses and prospers his people as he sees will best fulfil his will. For our part, even when the word of the kingdom falls on good soil, not all of us are equally submissive, obedient or willing to depend on him. And not all are equally hungry to gain godly knowledge, understanding and holiness of life. At another level, the fruitfulness of even the most faithful and diligent of us may be limited by our circumstances and by the situation in which the Lord has placed us. But our constant aim can be to be faithful and as fruitful as he enables us to be.

Conclusion
Matthew, Mark and Luke each record the parable of the sower. Although this parable is explored at some length in the earlier book *Exploring and Applying the Parables of Jesus in the Gospel of Luke*, it

is revisited here because it is a key parable in understanding the nature and purpose of the parables.

We like to critically assess what we hear – but Jesus' parables critically assess us! Jesus taught in parables to invite those hungry for the truth underlying them to explore their significance further. Only those with spiritual eyes open, 'ears to hear' and hearts receptive to the things of God would – and still will – do so.

The parable of the sower is a challenge and a tonic, both for those who hear or read the word of God and for those whose task and calling it is to 'sow' the word.

For those who hear or read the word, the challenge is to prayerfully think about its implications, and its application to our own lives. How can we put into practice and benefit from what we have learnt and understood. Over time, the word truly received bears fruit in godly repentance and faith, in godly living, and in godly service.

For those who preach or write, the challenge is to faithfully keep 'sowing', and draw encouragement from our Lord's own ministry, which by no means found the favour with the religious leaders of the day, and whose words seemed to fall on such a high proportion of hearers who were quite unmoved by them. Yet the Lord God was working his purpose out, and some 2000 years later there are millions of Christian believers word-wide whose lives have been totally transformed by 'the Son of God who loved us and gave himself for us' and who spent his life sowing the word of the kingdom in the lives of his disciples and of all who would truly hear him.

Heavenly father, give us ears to hear, and stir our hearts to long to understand your word, so that we may truly turn and be 'healed' – made whole people; forgiven and living in your world in a way that brings increasing honour to you and to your glorious and anointed Son who taught us this parable.

Questions for reflection or discussion

1. On reflection, have you ever found yourself with closed ears to the things of God? Do you know and pray for friends, colleagues and family members who are at present like that?

2. How easy is it for us to delight in 'the stories of Jesus', and in particular Jesus' parables, but like the great crowds pursue them no further?

3. Can we, too, be shallow rooted Christians? Can we identify with such times? How can we grow and deepen our own spiritual roots, and encourage the spiritual roots of our fellow believers to grow deeper?

4. Can we be depending on church leaders for the nurturing of our spiritual lives? Could this leave us totally unprepared for the difficulties and great knocks of life?

5. Are there times in life when the responsibilities we have at home and at work crowd in, and leave us little or no time or mental energy for quietness before the Lord God or usefulness before him? What are the danger signs? What can we do about them? How can we help one another in and through such times?

6. Can our natural interests, desires and abilities sometimes lead us astray from faithful discipleship and the Lord's best way for us?

7. How does fruitfulness before the Lord God lie in letting the teaching of our Lord become part of the fabric of our lives; setting our priorities and guiding our decisions?

8. 'The word truly received bears fruit in godly repentance and faith, in godly living, and in godly service.' Can you see what opportunities he has given to you to be fruitful? In what ways might we help one another to be fruitful before the Lord?

References

Watch and Pray – Mark 14:38
The disciples and those who were around him – Mark 4:10
Because seeing they do not see – Isaiah: 6:10

The shepherd of his people – Ezekiel 34:11-16

Visit and redeem his people – Zechariah's prophecy, Luke 1:67-80

Emmanuel, God among us Isaiah 7:14, 9:2, 6&7, 11:1-9

Simeon and Anna – Luke 2:25-38

The marks and signs of the true Messiah – Isaiah 35:3-6, 61:1-2

Tribulation – John 16:33, Acts 14:22, 2 Thessalonians 1:4

What shall we eat? – Matthew 6:25, 31-32

The word hidden in our hearts – Psalm 119:11

Bear fruit with patience – Luke 8:15

Loved us and gave himself for us – Galatians 2:20

The Growing Seed

The parable of the growing seed is one of a group of parables Jesus taught the crowds concerning the nature and growth the kingdom of God. The group includes the sower, the lamp on a stand, the mustard seed and the leaven. Within this group of parables, only Mark records the parable of the growing seed and it is set in the place where Matthew and Luke record the parable of the leaven. This presents us with no difficulty as Jesus taught in parables, one after another in rapid succession and the Gospel writers have been selective in what they have recorded.

The Growing Seed
"If anyone has ears to hear, let him hear." And he said to them, "Pay attention to what you hear: with the measure you use, it will be measured to you, and still more will be added to you. For to the one who has, more will be given, and from the one who has not, even what he has will be taken away."

And he said, "The kingdom of God is as if a man should scatter seed on the ground. He sleeps and rises night and day, and the seed sprouts and grows; he knows not how. The earth produces by itself, first the blade, then the ear, then the full grain in the ear. But when the grain is ripe, at once he puts in the sickle, because the harvest has come."

And he said, "With what can we compare the kingdom of God, or what parable shall we use for it? It is like a grain of mustard seed, which when sown in the ground, is the smallest of all the seeds on earth, yet when it is sown it grows up and becomes larger than all the garden plants and puts out large branches, so that the birds of the air can make nests in its shade."

With many such parables he spoke the word to them, as they were able to hear it. He did not speak to them without a parable, but privately to his own disciples he explained everything.

Mark 4:23-34 English Standard Version

The Growing Grain

The setting of the parable
As a countryman, Jesus often drew his illustrations from the natural world, just as the apostle Paul, a man of the city, so often drew his illustrations from races, competitions and soldiers.

In the parable of the sower Jesus had warned his hearers about the different levels of hearing – from those completely 'deaf' to the word, to those in whose life the word was stifled by great difficulty or the pleasures and cares of this world, to those in whose life the word of God was fruitful.

Mark records that, before Jesus began this parable of the seed growing, he reinforced that warning, "Pay attention to what you hear: with the measure you use, it will be measured to you, and still more will be added to you. For to the one who has, more will be given, and from the one who has not, even what he has will be taken away."

To attentive and spiritually awakened hearers, the parables lit up the nature of the kingdom of God. However, to those merely enjoying hearing his stories – but with no willingness to ponder what he was saying – Jesus' parables only entertained them for the moment. They had 'no ears to hear' the spiritual truths of the kingdom of God.

"The kingdom of God is as if a man should scatter seed on the ground . . ."

The farmer centuries ago may not have known the details of the biochemistry of the processes of germination and growth as he scattered his seed. However, he knew by his own experience, and by the long experience of former generations, that if seeds of grain are sown in prepared ground they will produce a harvest.

Growth to maturity takes time and so, having sown the seed, the farmer goes about his other normal daily business confident that the seed will grow. 'He sleeps and rises night and day, and the seed sprouts and grows; he knows not how. The earth produces by itself, first the blade, then the ear, then the full grain in the ear. But when the grain is ripe, at once he puts in the sickle, because the harvest has come.'

The farmer does not 'make' the seed grow. As any gardener will tell you, the most he can do is make the conditions for growth as favourable as possible by preparing the soil, sowing the seed and then weeding, fertilising, watering and protecting the crop from frosts and pests.

Although modern agriculture increases the favourableness of the conditions for a harvest, this does not modify the fundamental God-given and amazing processes of germination and growth.

'The earth produces by itself first the blade . . .' The Greek word for 'produces by itself' is the word from which we get the word 'automatically' and we use it when something or someone is doing what it has been designed or trained to do.

Like the seed of mustard, the grain has life in itself and, once sown, can be left to do its own work according to the Creator's design. In due time, given favourable conditions, the seeds will produce a harvest.

Until harvest time, the farmer can relax and be busy about other things. 'He sleeps and rises night and day, and the seed sprouts and grows . . .' However, 'when the grain is ripe, at once he puts in the sickle, because the harvest has come.'

In what ways is this parable a picture of the kingdom of God?
The kingdom of God is the Lord God's rule and reign in the hearts and lives of people. By fallen human nature we live in God's world as if there were no God before whom – whether we choose to acknowledge it or not – we shall each be called to give account for the one life given to us. Ignoring the One in whose hand is our existence and all the circumstances of our life is a huge mistake A mistake which can only lead to our being finally swept away in judgement.

We will never know forgiveness, and the fullness of life God intended for us, until we submit to him, honour and obey him. This is the essence of the kingdom of God, the rule of God in his world.

"The kingdom of God is as if a man should scatter seed . . ."
We need to ask two questions. What seed is sown to produce a harvest for the kingdom of God? And what is the mechanism by which the 'seed' of the kingdom is planted in hearts and minds?

The answer must be the word of God, first sown by the faithful prophets of the Old Testament, then by Lord Jesus himself and then, in their turn, by his chosen apostles, and by faithful 'heralds of God', preachers and teachers through the running centuries. Like seed scattered, the word of God produces a harvest. It does not do so instantly, but quietly and over a period of time.

Like seed sown in the ground, some of the seeds will fail to produce mature grain and some will flourish and be very fruitful. It is like that with the word of God when it has been sown, as our Lord explored and explained in the parable of the sower.

How did the disciples understand the parable and learn from it?
The Lord's own priority was preaching and teaching and he illustrated and accompanied this with very practical help for the sick and suffering and spiritually captive people of his day.

After Jesus' resurrection and the Day of Pentecost, the disciples clearly saw themselves as charged with 'sowing the seed of God's kingdom'. Their whole lives were to be spent in preaching, teaching and writing. Like their Lord, the ministry of the apostles was accompanied by signs and wonders.

Empowered by the Holy Spirit, Peter was the first to proclaim the Gospel of God to both the Jews and to the Gentiles. He proclaimed it to the Jewish people who had come to Jerusalem for the feast of Pentecost, and later he was called of God to proclaim that same Gospel to the Gentile people gathered in the house of the God-fearing Roman, Cornelius.

In the same way, the word of God was faithfully sown by the apostle Paul. By preaching, debating, arguing and pleading and writing, he proclaimed the Gospel and it clearly bore fruit in a great many hearts and lives, just as seed sown in receptive soil produces a harvest.

Are the results of faithfully sowing of God's word instant?
Again the parable is instructive. Like the growing grain producing 'first the blade, then the ear, then the full grain in the ear,' spiritual growth is all but unnoticed from day to day. Growth to spiritual maturity takes place over time – as it did with the disciples. As Jesus taught them over a period of three years, the disciples gradually grew to understand more of the ways of God. Even after years of being with the Lord, their understanding was far from complete. Like ours, their minds had been filled with many popular misunderstandings and false assumptions.

There were highlights, for example, when Peter confessed the Lord Jesus to be the promised Messiah, the Son of God. But there were also many times of faltering, for example, when the disciples all fled at the arrest of Jesus or when Peter denied he even knew Jesus.

After Pentecost the Holy Spirit continued to do his sovereign work in bringing to mind and showing the disciples the significance of more and more of the things Jesus had done and taught them.

It is just the same today. We may enter the kingdom of heaven, 'be born again from above' and filled with zeal for the kingdom of heaven in a moment, but we are not born 'instantly mature'. Like the first disciples, we too are 'slow to grasp all the prophets have written', yet over the years it is thrilling to see the word of our Lord and the Holy Spirit doing this wonderful work of spiritual growth in individual lives. Men, women and young people can be seen to be 'growing in grace and in the knowledge of our Lord' as the apostle Peter puts it.

Even then, like the grain in its growth, the growth of grace in the heart and its effect on the daily life we are living, may be very gradual; godliness of living growing little by little and stage by stage – 'first the blade, then the ear, after that the full corn in the ear'.

We do not need to know the detailed mechanism of individual spiritual growth. Of us it can be truthfully said, 'we know not how'. But, like the apostle Paul, we can be confident that, 'he who has begun a good work . . . will bring it to completion.'

The parable is a picture of the sowing of the word of God in the minds, hearts and lives of those who will hear. It is by the faithful sowing of the word of God and by its receptive hearing that the kingdom of God is planted and grows.

Spiritual growth – the part that is ours to play

Once sown, seeds 'automatically' feed themselves on the water and nutrients in the soil. However, many Christian people do not do that for themselves. It is too easy to depend on 'pre-wrapped spiritual snacks' and an occasional or maybe weekly 'meal' from a church or chapel service to keep us spiritually fit and growing. It is a rare church that can truly nourish spiritual growth.

Like the seeds, we will be far more likely to grow to mature fruitfulness as we daily feed ourselves from the 'soil' of the Scriptures. Guided by the Holy Spirit, as we read and re-read the Scriptures, we will grow in godly wisdom, understanding and practice. Prayer and time spent with the God-given Scriptures are like the earth in the parable, 'The earth produces by itself, first the blade, then the ear, then the full grain in the ear.'

Here is a challenge to us to make sure that we are growing in godly knowledge and maturity. Only in this way will we be prepared for the Lord God's harvest, at the end of our life, or at the end of the age when the final harvest of the earth takes place.

The part we can actively play in 'sowing the word'
The parable is also a challenge sow faithfully as the Lord gives us the opportunities. We can sow the word by sharing a godly word as we help someone, by giving or lending a godly book or booklet, by inviting a friend or colleague to a gathering where the Gospel seed will be publicly sown and the Scriptures clearly explained.

As with the seed sown, so it is with the 'seed' of the word of God. The person who proclaims, shares or 'sows' it, has a vital part to play, but it is limited to having confidence in the power of God's word and the work of the Holy Spirit in the lives of those who hear. Despite the feebleness of the sower, behind the word of God faithfully sown is the power of God to bring men and women to repentance before God and to fruitful faith in the Lord Jesus.

A warning, lest those who sow the word are surprised or discouraged
It is salutary to note that many of our Lord's own words fell on spiritually deaf ears, producing no lasting repentance towards God . The apostle Paul, as he sowed the word among his fellow Jewish people, found the same to be true. Many hearts were hardened and ears unreceptive. Sadly, this has been the case with the God-given words sown by faithful ministers and teachers down the years.

It is very humbling simply to be a sower of the word of God, and to leave the resulting harvest to the sovereign working of God the Holy Spirit. Like the man in the Lord's parable who 'knows not how,' it is not for the one who sows to choose who, or when, or whether a hearer may be brought to true, lasting and spiritually fruitful faith. The task is simply to faithfully sow.

The parable's relevance to those called to public ministry
On a wider scale, in each generation the Lord has been calling preachers and teachers, ministers and writers to sow his word, and to do so as widely as he gives them opportunity.

John Calvin comments that here is a word of encouragement from our Lord to those who sow the word of God. One can become discouraged by the lack of visible results. Yet, like the farmer who has faithfully sown his seed, we are not to be discouraged or fretful if we do not see instant results, let alone give up the task of sowing. Those who sow the word of God are to faithfully sow, and then go about the rest of their daily business in the knowledge that the Lord God will not let his word return to him void, but will accomplish his sovereign purposes.

The harvest of such labour is secure, even if, like seed beneath the soil, its development in the earliest stages is all but imperceptible, long delayed and secret. The seed of the word of God has often been seen to lie dormant for decades in a person's life. But then, perhaps triggered by some event, it has sprung to life.

Matthew Henry comments that the growth of the seed is wonderfully free from need of human attention – the farmer rests and goes about his other business. So it is with the working of the Holy Spirit as he opens eyes to the kingdom of God and the word of God. The Holy Spirit enlightens the mind to the truth of God's word, stirs the heart and will to turn from living for ourselves to living in God's world in a way that pleases him.

However, there is no encouragement here for pastors or fellow believers to neglect the growing grain, but rather that we can have confidence that, under the hand of God, the word faithfully sown will lead to a harvest.

The growth of the seed sown seen across the whole field
Individual seeds need to grow and develop. But for a harvest, the seeds in a whole field or area of land need to grow. So we need to explore

this process of growth both in individual people and across the whole of the Lord God's 'field'.

Enlightened and empowered by the Holy Spirit of God, what a harvest was brought in on the day of Pentecost as Peter faithfully proclaimed the Gospel. And among the Jewish people in the days following, 'the Lord added to the church daily those who were being saved'.

A little later the believers were scattered by persecution. As they searched for somewhere safe to live, they shared the Gospel with their non-Jewish neighbours, many of whom came to believe.

Barnabas, with the apostle Paul followed this up, first teaching and building up the church at Antioch, and then being sent by that church to 'sow the word' and plant churches throughout the Roman Empire. And so, on a larger scale, the kingdom of heaven spread from a few hundred Jewish believers to a great many Jewish and Gentile churches of believers scattered throughout the Roman Empire.

It has gone on growing. In the West, the church is generally failing – as societies we have turned our back on God and godly ways, but in the Eastern nations, despite persecution, the Christian church is flourishing. Even in our day, the Lord is adding to the church daily.

The final harvest of the people of God
Across the world, as each generation has been succeeded by the next through the running centuries, the seed of the word which our Lord first sowed has been quietly growing, developing and ripening. In each generation, Jesus' life and teaching has produced a harvest of people whose lives have been fruitful as they have trusted, loved, honoured and served him. These are the ones who, season by season, our Lord has already been gathering towards his harvest.

At the end of the age the Lord Jesus himself will return to gather in his final harvest and usher in the fulfilment of the kingdom of heaven. The believers living at that time will be gathered with believers who have lived in earlier times to be part of the Lord's final harvest home and this will mark the end of the world as we know it and the beginning of the reign of the Lord God and his Son.

Over the centuries, especially in times of great difficulty, many have yearned and cried for that day, 'even so come Lord Jesus.'

Heavenly Father we thank you for Mark recording this challenging parable which fell from the lips of your Son.

Questions for reflection or discussion

1. To live in God's world as if there were no God is a huge mistake. Why?
2. Many of our Lord's own words fell on spiritually deaf ears, producing no lasting repentance towards God or faith in his Son, and so have the God-given words of faithful ministers down the years. Why is this?
3. How can we usefully be sowing the word of God and helping the people around us?
4. Have you seen the word of our Lord and the Holy Spirit doing a wonderful work of spiritual growth in individual lives?
5. Is it enough for us to depend on 'spiritual snacks' and a weekly or occasional meal from a church or chapel service to keep us spiritually fit and growing?
6. How can we be 'growing in grace and in the knowledge of our Lord' as the apostle Peter puts it?
7. The seed of the word has often been seen to lie dormant for decades in a person's life. But then, perhaps triggered by some event, it has sprung to life. Have you seen or known that?

Footnotes
1. The significance of Mark's inclusion of this parable

Firstly, the parable of the growing grain is among a group of parables recorded by each of the first three Gospel writers, but this particular parable is found only in the Gospel of Mark, where it is followed by the parable of the mustard seed.

When teaching the disciples, Jesus spoke to them directly, explaining to them the ways of the kingdom of heaven and answering their questions. However, when teaching the great crowds of people who flocked to hear him, Jesus taught in pictures, one parable after the next.

Matthew and Luke do not record the parable of the growing grain, but in its place record the parable of the leaven. This is worthy of note, as it reflects the fact that Jesus used a great many parables as he taught, and the Gospel writers have each recorded a selection of them.

Secondly, the presence of the parable of the growing grain, paired by Mark with the parable of the mustard seed, makes it clear that both of these parables are concerned with hearing the word of God and with the growth of the kingdom of God.

This throws into serious question the quite widely held view that the parables of the sower, the leaven and the mustard seed are not about the growth of the kingdom of God, but are about the development of evil within the church. There is not a hint of anything that could be understood as representing evil in this parable of the growing grain.

2. A difficulty we can make for ourselves
J.C. Ryle comments, 'In this, as in many of our Lord's parables, we must carefully keep in view the main scope and object of the whole story, and not lay too much stress on lesser points.'

If we press the details of the parable too far, we will make difficulties for ourselves as Richard Trench explains. For example, if we ask, "Who is represented by the man who sowed the seed?" If we conclude that the Lord Jesus is the only sower of the grain, can it be true that 'the seed sprouts and grows; he knows not how' or that he plants and then leaves it, turns his back on it as he 'sleeps and rises night and day'?

If, on the other hand, we conclude that our Lord is referring not to himself but to his appointed ministers there are still difficulties, for it is not they, but the Lord of the harvest who will gather in the final harvest of the true people of God.

In the first case we are in danger of belittling the Lord, in the second we give too great a privilege to preachers and those who sow the word of God.

Perhaps it is most helpful to understand that our Lord is the master of the harvest, and those he calls through the centuries to sow God's word, are his servants and helpers in his harvest field.

References

In whose hand is our existence and all our circumstances – Daniel 5:23
Our Lord's own words fell on spiritually deaf ears – Luke 10:16
The Lord's own priority was preaching and teaching – Mark 1:35-39
The apostles' ministry was accompanied by signs and wonders – Hebrews 2:4
The word of God faithfully sown is the power of God – Romans 1:16
He who has begun a good work – Philippians 1:6
The Lord will not let his word return to him void – Isaiah 55:10-11
Born again from above – John 3:3a
Slow to grasp all the prophets have written – Luke 24:25
Growing in grace and in the knowledge of our Lord – 2 Peter 3:18.
The final harvest – Revelation 14:14-16
The Lord added to the church daily those who were being saved – Acts 2:47
Even so come Lord Jesus – Revelation 22:20

The Weeds Sown Among the Corn

He put another parable before them, saying, "The kingdom of heaven may be compared to a man who sowed good seed in his field, but while his men were sleeping, his enemy came and sowed weeds among the wheat and went away. So when the plants came up and bore grain, the weeds appeared also. And the servants of the master of the house came and said to him, 'Master, did you not sow good seed in your field? How then does it have weeds?' He said to them, 'An enemy has done this.' So the servants said to him, 'Then do you want us to go and gather them?' But he said, 'No, lest in gathering the weeds you root up the wheat along with them. Let both grow together until the harvest, and at harvest time I will tell the reapers, 'Gather the weeds first and bind them in bundles to be burned, but gather the wheat into my barn.'"

Matthew 13:24-30 English standard version

(The verses that follow record Jesus teaching the crowds of hearers the parables of the Mustard Seed and the Leaven and conclude with the comment, 'All these things Jesus said to them in parables . . .' After these verses, Matthew continues . . .)

Then he left the crowds and went into the house. And his disciples came to him, saying, "Explain to us the parable of the weeds of the field." He answered, "The one who sows the good seed is the Son of Man. The field is the world, and the good seed is the children of the kingdom. The weeds are the sons of the evil one, and the enemy who sowed them is the devil. The harvest is the close of the age, and the reapers are angels. Just as the weeds are gathered and burned with fire, so will it be at the close of the age. The Son of Man will send his angels, and they will gather out of his kingdom all causes of sin and all law-breakers*, and throw them into the fiery furnace. In that place there will be weeping and gnashing of teeth. Then the righteous will shine like the sun in the kingdom of their Father."

'He who has ears, let him hear.'

Matthew 13:36-43 English Standard Version

*Law-breakers is a literal translation of the Greek, it is a technical term and in this setting means all those ignoring the Lord God and his commandments.

The Weeds in the Field

C.H. Dodd sees the parable as Jesus' answer to something that was a puzzle and stumbling block to the Jewish leaders. How could Jesus claim that the kingdom of heaven had arrived – was 'among them', 'in the midst of them,' – when there were so many sinners in Israel? And, how could they recognise as God's anointed King one who, in their eyes was a 'nobody'; a mere self-appointed, crowd-raising, Sabbath-breaking rabbi from, of all places, Nazareth?

Jesus answered them by way of this parable, implying that the prophets and John the Baptist had prepared the Lord's 'field' and that he, the Lord Jesus, was both sowing and reaping the first fruits of the harvest of the kingdom of heaven. The first fruits were those who, in the apostle John's words, '. . . received him and believed on his name'. To these, and to these alone, was given the authority to be the sons and daughters of the kingdom of God. Those who 'received him' were those who recognised Jesus for who he was; Israel's true King, God's anointed One, their long expected Messiah. The religious leaders were stumbled because they could not, or would not, receive him in this way. They could not recognise either the kingdom of heaven when it was so 'contaminated' with sinners, or its King clothed in such humility.

Jesus was showing them who he truly was and that, until the final ingathering has taken place, the harvest field of the kingdom of heaven would always be mixed. There would be many apparent but false 'disciples' and much opposition, and there will always be sowing and harvesting taking place together. This is the way it has proved to be through the centuries.

The time of sowing
'The kingdom of heaven may be compared to a man who sowed good seed in his field, but while his men were sleeping, his enemy came and sowed weeds among the wheat and went away.'

'Then he left the crowds and went into the house. And his disciples came to him, saying, "Explain to us the parable of the weeds of the field." He answered, "The one who sows the good seed is the Son of Man. The field is the world, and the good seed is the children of the kingdom. The weeds are the sons of the evil one, and the enemy who sowed them is the devil.'

Although some of the more liberal modern scholars put aside the explanation of the parable as a later interpretation, it is clear that, when the Gospel as we have it was written, this is how the parable was understood. Matthew's Gospel itself records that it was given because the disciples asked Jesus to explain the parable. Speaking of the great crowds, Mark records, 'With many such parables he spoke the word to them, as they were able to hear it. He did not speak to them without a parable, but privately to his own disciples he explained everything.'

The good seed
Our Lord himself is like the man who sowed good seed. Jesus was constantly calling his hearers to repentance before God and to faith. He was calling people to submit, honour and obey the Lord God and to honour his anointed Son. Beginning with the disciples and those around them, the people who did so were made the children of the

kingdom of heaven. Their eyes were opened and they were 'born of the Holy Spirit of God'.

From our perspective, 2000 years later, we can see that the Lord has scattered his children all over the world, his 'field'. He has called them to serve him and bear fruit for him wherever he has put them; some in very difficult circumstances and some in very peaceful and happy ones. There is a spiritual and very wonderful fellowship between the children of the kingdom across the ages and across the globe, and the Lord will gather us all at his final harvest-time.

In the meantime we are called to support and encourage one another, as we are able.

Sadly, we can see that the enemy has also scattered his children through the world, both through society in general and through the Christian church.

The weeds

In the parable of the sower, the Lord has shown the great crowds, and explained to his disciples, the need to take great care how they hear if they are to be fruitful before him. In this parable Jesus explains privately to the disciples the opposition they must expect as they fulfill the great commission he was to give them, sowing the Gospel of God and tending the growing churches. It also stands as a warning to the people of God through the running centuries.

Jesus gives us a glimpse of the adversary, the enemy of God, and one of the enemy's strategies. He exposes the weedy field in which we live, for what it is – a world spoiled by the evil one.

To intermingle his counterfeit seed with the true and so cause maximum hurt to the farmer, John Chrysostom notes that the evil one sowed his seed when the field was freshly prepared, the good seed sown and the farmer and his men asleep. Typically, like a thief in the night – 'he came, he did his dark work, and he went'.

What seed was the enemy sowing? The word 'weeds' puts into our minds broad-leafed weeds like thistles and docks, but the word is better translated 'tares', a false crop, as broad-leafed 'weeds' would have been noticed far earlier than the time the true crop was beginning to bear grain.

There was one seed that the Romans made a criminal offence to plant in your neighbour's, competitor's or enemy's field. It was the rye grass, Bearded Darnel, or Poison Darnel, which as it grew looked like wheat. This rye grass, Bearded Darnel, would closely fit our Lord's description and so Jesus' hearers would immediately relate to the parable and understand it.

The time of growing

'So when the plants came up and bore grain, the weeds appeared also. And the servants of the master of the house came and said to him, 'Master, did you not sow good seed in your field? How then does it have weeds?' He said to them, 'An enemy has done this.' So the servants said to him, 'Then do you want us to go and gather them?' But he said, 'No, lest in gathering the weeds you root up the wheat along with them. Let both grow together until the harvest.'

As the crop was growing it would be all but impossible to distinguish between the weeds and the true crop. Only when the seed heads began to form and the harvest drew near, could the plants be distinguished. By then it was too late. The crop would be ruined – the roots entangled, and the true grain choked by the strongly competing weed. Any attempt to separate them would do more damage to the true crop than leaving them growing together until the harvest. Only then could they be safely separated.

Even worse than taking up space and competing for water and nutrients, Darnel, if that is the weed our Lord was referring to, is host to an assortment of rusts and the fungus ergot which causes infected ears of grain to greatly enlarge, become very dark in colour and poisonous. It can make people poisoned by it appear drunk and irrational, which is almost certainly the root of the common name Darnel, which means 'drunkenness'. The poison is similar to the hallucinogenic drug LSD and in sufficient quantity can kill both animals and humans.

Who are these enemy-sown people?
Among national leaders one can clearly see the benefits of nations led by godly and upright people. Sadly, we can also see the deception and destruction brought about in and by nations led by those of a very different persuasion. Stalin and Hitler and their modern equivalents were once among many lads growing up who were 'full of promise' and yet fully grown they caused great heartbreak and destruction.

Of the false crop in the church, Augustine laments that among the people gathered to the church, even among those holding the highest office in the church, '. . . there is both wheat, and tares.'

We have to be careful in putting labels on people. We are all made in the image of God, and are the objects of his love. It is not the will of the Lord God that any should suffer the fate described in the explanation of this parable, but that all should turn in repentance and faith and so become a part of the Lord's fruitful harvest crop.

By the grace of God, as Augustine observed, one who is a child of the evil one today, can become a child of God tomorrow. It was for this very purpose that the Son of Man came 'to give his life a ransom for many' and 'to seek and to save the lost.'

By human nature we do not find ourselves inclined to submit to our Maker. Motivated by our own desires, the opinions of the world around us, and, perhaps unconsciously, under the influence of the evil one, we have an inbuilt unwillingness to submit to our heavenly Father's commands and fatherly instructions. Our natural human pride also makes it hard for us to accept the necessity of the cross of his Son to pay the ransom for our forgiveness of such rebellion against our Maker. As the Scriptures make clear, because of our human pride and unwillingness to submit to the Lord God and his Son, we are not by nature the children of the kingdom of heaven.

Even our convinced opinion of ourselves, of our actions and of our standing before him may be terribly mistaken – as was the case with Saul, the devoted and highly religious Pharisee, who 'laid waste the church' yet believed he was acting in God's cause. Imprisonments and labour camps, beheadings and burnings at the stake, only follow Saul's terrible pattern of devilish weeds tangling the roots and attempting to choke the true grain of the kingdom of heaven.

But note well, the apostle Paul is a wonderful example of Augustine's warning not to be hasty in our judgment, as those who are 'weed' one day can become 'wheat' the next. Here is Saul, a man determined to choke and destroy believers, who after his encounter with the risen Lord Jesus, became Paul, one of the Lord's most effective advocates.

Among the churches that the apostle Paul planted there were very active and vigorous 'weeds,' some are described by him as 'false apostles, deceitful workers'. In G.H. Lang's words they, 'fashion themselves to be ministers of righteousness, as Satan can fashion himself as an angel of light.' They hinder the harvest and draw followers into sects, and are often 'brilliant in scholarship, pleasant in manner, suave in speech' yet they are not the sons of the kingdom of heaven but of the enemy. And 'usually they have done their deadly work before it can be recognised by the many.'

G.H. Lang also comments, 'The enemy did not long delay his attack. Already among the apostolic twelve . . . he found in Judas his traitorous agent. In only the second Christian church Simon Magnus appears. Paul had scarcely left Corinth when 'faction-makers arose.' It was not long before 'false brethren . . . crept in secretly.' As Jesus warned the disciples by this parable, the false crop was sown from the very beginning. It has been sown in every season in the church and in the world, including our own times.

Do you want us to go and gather them?
Our Lord clearly taught, by way of this parable, that his kingdom here on earth would be mixed, the true and the false growing together until the final harvest. Nevertheless, like the servants of the parable, we are often impatient to sort the true from the false, and to do so long before the final harvest.

Throughout the centuries there have been many attempts to separate the weeds from the wheat; the true sons and daughters of God from the children of the evil one. But our Lord's concern is for the well-being of his sons and daughters, his harvest crop, and for their fruitfulness, and so the owner of the field restrains his servants because of the damage such separation brings.

The relevance of our Lord's warning
In our own day, both from the world and within the church, there seems to be a very deep-seated determination to 'weed out' or stifle those who have a simple and obedient devotion to the One who told this parable, and who long to conform their lives to the Lord God's commandments and fatherly instructions found in the Scriptures.

Sown in the visible church, the false, to secure their own position, will inevitably deny that there is any distinction to be made, 'We are all followers of Jesus' and 'all is well'. However, at the same time, they will often attempt to suppress, exclude and rid the church of the true sons and daughters of God.

On the other side of the coin, attempts by the true children of the kingdom to throw out those whose faith they question, or to grow and keep a 'pure' church, have not been successful or happy either. It is well to take note of the teaching of this parable, and recognise that in this world the Lord's visible kingdom will always be very mixed. Even one generation being succeeded by the next in the visible church can bring this about.

However, the parable does not undermine our Lord's teaching regarding discipline in the church. It is clear from the New Testament that the disciples took note of Jesus' teaching and, together with the apostle Paul, took great care as they wrote letters and visited the churches they had planted, encouraging them, warning them or calling individuals and whole churches to repent.

In the meantime the parable is a call to recognise what is going on and, despite the enemy's tactics, be prayerfully determined to be fruitful both individually and as a body of believers.

The time of harvest

For our encouragement, we are taught to keep an eye on the coming harvest time.

> 'Let both grow together until the harvest, and at harvest time I will tell the reapers, 'Gather the weeds first and bind them in bundles to be burned, but gather the wheat into my barn.'
>
> 'The harvest is the close of the age, and the reapers are angels. Just as the weeds are gathered and burned with fire, so will it be at the close of the age. The Son of Man will send his angels, and they will gather out of his kingdom all causes of sin and all law-breakers [those ignoring the Lord God and his commandments], and throw them into the fiery furnace. In that place there will be weeping and gnashing of teeth. Then the righteous will shine like the sun in the kingdom of their Father.'

As Jesus' first hearers would have been well aware, at harvest we gather and store all we want and grew the crop for. It will be like that at the end of the age. At God's appointed time, a declaration will be made, 'the harvest is ready' and the order given to 'gather in his chosen'. Then the Son of Man will send his angels to gather his final harvest.

Harvest marks the completion of growth and the final gathering of the true crop.

The final destiny of the false 'disciples'

Note well the terrible warning and punishment facing those who fail to humbly honour and obey the Lord God, and those who mislead, mistreat or attempt to eliminate his true sons and daughters.

The angelic servants of the Lord of the harvest 'will gather out of his kingdom all causes of sin;' those who by their teaching and lifestyle undermine true faith and godly living in others. 'And all lawbreakers' – those who live in God's world as if there were no God and so take no notice of his commandments and fatherly instructions.

Archbishop Richard Trench writes, '. . . the terrible doom of ungodly men under the image of the burning with fire . . . is frequent in Scripture. Whatever 'the furnace of fire' may mean here, – or the 'lake of fire' of Revelation 19:20 and 20:10, or the 'fire that is not quenched' Mark 9:48, the 'everlasting fire' Matthew 25:41, – this at all events is certain; that they point to some doom so intolerable that the Son of God came down from heaven and tasted all the bitterness of death, that He might deliver us from ever knowing the secrets of anguish . . . shut up in these terrible words: "There shall be wailing and gnashing of teeth."'

The final destiny of the true sons and daughters of God

These two final destinies are almost certainly a reflection of the prophecy of Daniel: 'And many of those who sleep in the dust of the earth shall awake, some to everlasting life, and some to everlasting shame and everlasting contempt. And those who are wise shall shine like the brightness of the sky above; and those who turn many to righteousness, like the stars for ever and ever.'

'Then the righteous will shine like the sun in the kingdom of their Father.'

At the time of his transfiguration the Lord Jesus' hidden glory was openly to be seen. The children of the kingdom will be like their Lord. They, too, will share his glory and shine like the sun.

Here is the wonderful vindication and reward of those who are truly his people and are seeking with all their mind and heart and effort to be fruitful for him in this sometimes very hard and difficult world.

Only on the Last Day will the true children of the kingdom be seen to be those most to be envied, the sons and daughters of the living God. Until then, they will find themselves mixed among the people of the world, and often, like their Master, they will be despised and rejected.

In summary

The parable is a picture of the Lord God's business in the world. He is pictured as being like a farmer. He has made and prepared his field – the world. Season by season, he is sowing, growing and harvesting and will finally gather in his crop. What is his crop? – People: People who will bring glory to his name, who will love, honour, and obey him, and people who will hear and obey his anointed Son, the One who told this parable.

This great and glorious Farmer has an inveterate enemy who through the running seasons is also sowing a crop, a crop designed to frustrate and entangle the Lord God's crop and in every way impoverish the Farmer.

How should the children of the kingdom live?

– With a clear vision of being fruitful for the Lord God.

– With a clear understanding of the difficulties, frustrations, opposition and setbacks we shall face if we are determined to glorify God and his Son in this world.

– Aware that there is a final, absolutely just but terrible, separation between the 'sons of the kingdom' and 'the sons of the enemy.'

– Constantly keeping in mind the glory that awaits 'the good and faithful servant' who is about his Master's business and so fruitful before him.

Heavenly Father, open our eyes and help us to be watchful, wary and aware of the fact that in this world you, and those who are yours, have a very determined, skillful and subtle enemy. Open our eyes to see the world and the visible church for what it is, 'a weedy field', and despite all, to strive in the power of the Holy Spirit to be fruitful before you.

A footnote on 'weeding'

An example of mistaken 'weeding' would be the 'weeding out' of the people who discovered the apostolic faith from the English translation of the Gospels by John Wycliffe, 'the morning star of the reformation.' He was an Oxford professor of theology who lived from about 1320-1384. Wycliffe was hated and hounded because he came to see that Scripture, rather than the traditions of the church, was the only authoritative and reliable guide to the true knowledge of God and godly ways. As a result he determined to put the Scriptures into the hands of the ordinary people.

Wycliffe's translation of the New Testament from the Latin into English enabled people to read the Scriptures and understand its teaching for themselves. In the century that followed, those whose faith was anchored in Wycliffe's English translation, rather than the teachings of the church, encouraged one another to learn by heart, recite and teach others, passages of the New Testament. They did so because this was before the invention of the printing press, and copies of the handwritten text were rare and precious. However, they were regarded as drunken, hallucinating heretics – weeds – and labelled, 'Lollards'. The label was most probably rooted in the Roman name for darnel, *lolium*, a rye grass thought to be the 'tares' or 'weeds' of the Bible which if infected can have drug-like properties. Hated and hounded by the church authorities, every attempt was made to violently 'weed them out'.

Questions for personal reflection or discussion

1. What caused the Pharisees to have such difficulty in accepting either Jesus or his message? What kind of characteristics were they expecting the Messiah to have?
2. Is it always easy for the children of the kingdom to be fruitful? Can the circumstances in which we find ourselves sometimes make that very difficult? (For example a dominating atheistic or religious state, or a very hostile culture at work or in our home, or even our television viewing)
3. Have you ever had to face opposition, competition and the stifling of godly living, speaking and fruitfulness? Who is the root of such difficulties?
4. 'While his men were asleep,' what opportunities do we give the evil one to do his dark work, or hide his destructive seed, in our own lives, in our families, in our church?
5. How are we in practice to be patient, maintain discipline in the church, but not to attempt to create, or to find, a 'pure' church?
6. How can we be alert to 'those who by their teaching and lifestyle undermine true faith and godly living in others'?
7. Are you concerned that so many around us 'live in God's world as if there were no God and so take no notice of his commandments and fatherly instructions'? How can we be fruitful among them?
8. Only on the Last Day will the true children of the kingdom be seen to be those most to be envied. For yourself and for those around you, do you labour for, and long to hear words like, 'Well done, good and faithful servant . . . enter into the joy of your lord.'?

References

The kingdom of heaven had arrived, was 'in the midst of them' – Luke 17:20-21 (See also, The kingdom of heaven is at hand – Matthew 3:2,

The kingdom of God has come near – Luke 10:9, 21:31, The kingdom of God has come upon you – Luke 11:20)
Those who received him – John 1:11-12
Privately to his own disciples he explained everything – Mark 4:33-34
Born of the Holy Spirit of God – John 3:3
The great commission – Matthew 28:18-20
Saul, determined to choke and destroy believers – Acts 8:3, 9:1-15
Simon Magnus – Acts 8:18-24
False brethren . . . crept in secretly – Galatians 2:4
Jesus' teaching about discipline in the church – Matthew 18:15-20
Paul's teaching about discipline in the church – 1Corinthians 5:1-5
God will 'gather in his chosen' – Matthew 24:30-31
It will be declared 'the harvest is ready' – Revelation 14:15
A reflection of the prophecy of Daniel – Daniel 12:2-3
The transfiguration – Matthew 17:1-8
Children of the kingdom like their Lord – 1 John 3:2
Well done, good and faithful servant – Matthew 25:21

The Hidden Treasure and the Pearl of Great Value

Again the kingdom of heaven is like treasure hidden in a field, which a man found and covered up. Then in his joy he goes and sells all he has and buys that field.

Again, the kingdom of heaven is like a merchant in search of fine pearls, who on finding one of great value, went and sold all that he had and bought it.

Matthew 13:44-46 English Standard Version

Introduction

These parables are only found in Matthew's Gospel. They clearly stand together and carry the same central message. It is the supreme value to be placed on being made a citizen of the kingdom of heaven. There is nothing of greater value. To bring his message home to the minds of his hearers, Jesus reinforced it by telling not one, but a pair of parables.

What is the kingdom of heaven?

From the first three lines of the prayer our Lord taught his disciples, it is clear that the kingdom of heaven is where the Lord's name is held in high regard, feared and revered, and where his will is perfectly, willingly and joyfully done.

We can have a foretaste of it in this present life – in as much as we willingly submit to the rule of the Lord God and live in glad obedience to his commandments and fatherly instructions – and in as much as we are willing to live in harmony with one another and with this beautiful but spoiled planet in which he has set us.

It is plain that a company of believing people should be living, and offering as a pattern to others, a foretaste of the kingdom of heaven. Tertullian could quote the unbelieving people living around him in North Africa saying, 'see how these Christians love one another', and he added, 'for they themselves hate one another.'

How do we enter the kingdom of heaven?
Some, like the man in the parable stumbling on treasure, gain entry into the kingdom of heaven by an apparent chance happening. Augustine, who, though he had been hungry for years, entered the kingdom this way. Augustine was deeply troubled and sat down on a bench under a fig tree. He heard a child's voice from a nearby house repeating or singing 'tolle, lege, tolle, lege,' 'take up and read, take up and read,' which stuck Augustine as word from the Lord for him, so he took up the New Testament and as he read, the Holy Spirit touched him and he became a new creation.

Others, like the merchant in the parable, enter the kingdom during the course of the most diligent searching and study. Martin Luther sought peace with God through many self-humiliating acts of penance but ultimately found it as he studied the apostle Paul's letter to the Romans. He discovered that the gateway to the kingdom is not penance but faith in the Son of God, the one who told these parables.

A free gift, yet worth everything else put together
The man discovering the treasure and the merchant with the pearl each went and sold all that they had to make their discoveries their own possession. The value of buried treasure or a priceless pearl is very great, even when it remains undiscovered. Yet, only when discovered is their true value appreciated. In the same way, membership of the kingdom of heaven is a great but hidden possession, and only when discovered, is it seen to be worth everything else put together.

The apostles, including Paul, demonstrated this great truth throughout their lives. The disciples left their fishing. Peter could say to Jesus, 'We have left everything and followed you,' and they continued to do so to the end of their lives. The apostle Paul counted as nothing his achievements as a Pharisee, writing, 'But whatever gain I had, I counted as loss for the sake of Christ. Indeed, I count everything as loss because of the surpassing worth of knowing Christ Jesus my Lord, for his sake I have suffered the loss of all things and count them as rubbish in order that I may gain Christ . . .'

They were willing to loosen their grasp on everything else in order to follow and serve their Lord. They faced being despised as ignorant and unlearned men, slandered with false accusations, whipped, imprisoned, even stoned and left for dead. All this was for the King and the kingdom's sake.

For ourselves, John Calvin notes that these two parables teach that those who would enter the kingdom of heaven must be willing to seek that above all else, so that nothing hinders us from obtaining it.

Matthew Henry writes, 'Those who would have a saving interest in Christ, must be willing to part with all for him, leave all to follow him. Whatever stands in opposition to Christ, or in competition with him for our love and service, we must cheerfully quit it, though ever so dear to us.'

We need such warnings because this world's possessions and opportunities are clearly to be seen and handled, whereas the kingdom of heaven is, for the present, secret and hidden.

However, describing being part of his kingdom as 'life', Jesus taught pictorially that it is worth losing eye, a hand, all this world's possessions, even life itself, rather than fail to obtain citizenship of the kingdom of heaven.

Here is the cost of the kingdom of heaven. It cannot be ours until we are willing to put all else in second place. This does not mean that we must fail to enjoy all that the Lord God provides for us in this beautiful world. But it does mean that we must live very lightly to them, seeking in first place the kingdom of heaven – prayerfully considering where we go, what we watch, what we do and what we say.

Here is the paradox. To enter the kingdom of heaven we must be willing to pay the fullest price to secure what is ultimately the free gift of God – the greatest treasure of all.

Treasure passed by
The world in general passed by the treasure hidden in a field. Their eyes were not open to the possibility, and so they were not keeping a look-out. Many a scientific discovery has been made but passed over as being of no significance – until someone with an awareness of its potential significance pursues it.

The treasure was only known to be of great value and worth everything else, when the man had found and seen it. Similarly, it took a skilful merchant to recognise the true value of that particular pearl, although it was freely on offer for sale to anyone. In the same way, the world just does not recognise the value of the kingdom of heaven and certainly would not be willing to lay everything else aside to obtain it.

The detail of the parable of the treasure found in a field
For us, the man's behaviour, as re-buries the treasure and secures it for himself, presents some difficulties. Arthur Carr comments, 'The dishonesty of the purchaser must be excluded from the thought of the parable.' That is surely right. Concentrating on the apparent sharp practice of the man as he buried the treasure and prepared to buy the field, we can easily tangle ourselves with our modern sensibilities, ideas, laws and practices, and so fail to understand the great teaching of the parable.

The legal right of the finder to own the treasure he discovered can be argued from Rabbinic teaching and law of the time. And so William Barclay writes, 'Although this parable sounds strange and unusual to us, it would sound perfectly natural to people in Palestine in the days of Jesus, and even to this day it would paint a picture which the people of the East would know well.'

In very unsettled times and countries, people have always buried their most precious possessions in order to keep them safe for recovery when a time of peace comes. If they do not survive, or are in some way unable to do so, and their family has no knowledge of its whereabouts, the treasure remains buried until some stranger discovers it.

Do note the joy of the man on discovering the treasure. When we really discover, or are discovered by, the kingdom of heaven there is great joy. The kind of joy Jesus pictured in the parable of the straying sheep brought safely home, the woman on finding her lost coin, and the joy of the father over the safe return of his son from a far country.

The detail of the parable of the pearl of great value
Matthew Henry points out that many of us are seeking something we regard as very desirable. For some that is the pursuit of wealth, for others the pursuit of honour and great learning or, like many who enter politics, for power and influence. For yet others it is the pursuit of sporting prowess, or fame, or pleasure. But here in this parable our Lord sets before us the pearl of greatest value; a pearl of everlasting value.

William Barclay finds this parable very telling, for just as the merchant was aware that there are many pearls, but nothing to compare with the one he had just found, so it is with the kingdom of heaven. There are many lovely things we can collect and treasure, and many good ways in which we can spend our lives. But nothing compares with the joy and satisfaction of living in this world as a member of the kingdom of heaven; of devoting ourselves to the love and service of the One who told this parable. He is the King, and as the apostle Paul makes plain, to spend our lives devoted to his service is this world's highest calling. However, to our great loss, the kingdom of heaven, this priceless pearl, is passed over by millions in our secular Western society.

Knowledge of the kingdom of heaven
The merchant was well informed concerning pearls, and so recognised the true value of this priceless pearl. In our present secular society, true knowledge of the ways of God and the Christian faith is denied to so many of the rising generation. Because, to a great extent, it is excluded from our schools and from the media, it is now possible to go through life totally uninformed of our responsibility before God in whose world we live, and totally uninformed of his merciful provision of forgiveness and peace with himself through the cross of his Son.

Even our modern churches and their leaders, when given a platform, rarely proclaim the Gospel of God; the kingdom of heaven and how to enter it – preferring to speak on green issues, commenting on political decisions, or speaking of 'living together in peace'.

Unlike previous generations, this generation simply does not know about the kingdom of heaven, this world's greatest joy and treasure, and without that knowledge, as Solomon's wise saying warns, they will 'run loose,' cast off restraint and head for ruin.

Knowledge of, and a heart's desire and hunger to become a member of the kingdom of heaven, coupled with a willingness to seriously engage with Scripture, can prepare us for this world's greatest discovery. Yet even the most painstaking seeking of the Lord and his kingdom needs to be coupled with earnest prayer that the Lord God would open our eyes to see the kingdom, for without the Holy Spirit's enabling, as Jesus said to Nicodemus, we cannot see the kingdom of God.

To the disciples who seriously wanted to know why Jesus taught in parables and what they meant, Jesus said, 'To you it is given to know the secrets of the kingdom of heaven, but [to those who just enjoyed his parables as stories] it has not been given.'

Is the parable a picture of the Lord's own mission on earth?
Our Lord was all of a piece, totally integrated. What he taught others, he practised himself. And so it is not surprising to find reflections of

Jesus' teaching practised in this life. For this reason, Christian eyes have seen in the parable of the merchant seeking fine pearls, a picture of our Lord seeking and rescuing his lost people. The Bible makes plain that the Lord God's treasure, his joy and jewels, are his people.

The apostle Paul, as he writes of the marriage bond, writes, '...as Christ loved the church and gave himself for it.' And as the twelfth chapter of the letter to the Hebrews makes plain, it was 'for the joy set before him' that the Lord Jesus suffered the loss of all things for his people. It is Scriptures such as these that enable both parables to also be understood as a picture of Jesus giving his all, even his life, for his people.

Conclusion

These two parables set before his hearers, and before ourselves in our day, the incomparable value of being a citizen of the kingdom of heaven. There is no greater joy or privilege than discovering who the Lord Jesus truly is, believing on him, trusting him, obeying him and being made a new creature; born again, by the Holy Spirit of God. This, and this alone, makes us a member of the family of God and a citizen of his kingdom. No earthly treasure, or priceless possession can compare with this, it is more precious than anything else.

However, the parables also call us to recognise that being a true member of the kingdom of God costs us our claim on everything else.

Heavenly father, by your Holy Spirit open our eyes to see the kingdom of heaven, to long to be a member of it and to be willing to give our all for the privilege of living in this world and the next as one of your chosen people.

Questions for personal reflection or discussion

1. How natural is for us to 'willingly submit to the rule of the Lord God and live in glad obedience to his commandments and fatherly instructions'?

2. How can we encourage one another to 'live in harmony with one another and with this beautiful but spoiled planet in which he has set us'?

3. A fellowship of believing people can, and should be, a reflection of the kingdom of heaven. In what ways can we help one another do better?

4. How easy is it to for us to follow the disciples' pattern of seeking in first place the kingdom of heaven, and willing to put all else in second place?

5. Unlike previous generations, today's young people simply do not know about the kingdom of heaven, this world's greatest joy and treasure, and without that knowledge, as Solomon's wise saying warns, they will 'run loose' and head for ruin. What can we do about it?

6. Christian eyes have seen in the parable of the merchant seeking fine pearls, a picture of our Lord seeking and rescuing his lost people. Do you find this a helpful secondary understanding of the parable?

Footnote

A note of caution. The man who discovered the treasure, and the merchant who found the pearl, sold everything to own or buy them, but there is no hint in the New Testament that we can in any way 'buy,' earn or merit a place in the kingdom of heaven. Its value is immense, but its membership is entirely the free gift of God. However, it is useful to consider the question 'In what ways do people, mistakenly, attempt to do so?'

References

Citizens of the kingdom of heaven – John:12-13 and John 3:5-8
The kingdom of heaven is a free gift of God – Romans 6:23
We have left everything and followed you – Matthew 19:27
The surpassing worth of knowing Christ Jesus – Philippians 3:7-8
Despised as ignorant and unlearned men – Acts 4:13
Slandered, whipped, imprisoned – Acts 16:19-24
Stoned and left for dead – Acts 14:19
Worth losing eye, a hand – Matthew 18:8-9, Matthew 16:24-26
The lost sheep, the lost coin, and the joy of the father – Luke 15:3-24.
This world's highest calling – Philippians 3:7-8
To you it is given to know the secrets of the kingdom of heaven – Matthew 13:11, Mark 4:10-11, Luke 8:9-10.
Solomon, they will 'run loose' and head for ruin – Proverbs 29:18
Without the Holy Spirit, we cannot see the kingdom – John 3:3.
The Lord God's people are his treasure – Malachi 3:16-17
As Christ loved the church and gave himself for it – Ephesians 5:25
For the joy set before him – Hebrews 12:2

The Net of Fish

"Again, the kingdom of heaven is like a net that was thrown into the sea and gathered fish of every kind. When it was full, men drew it ashore and sat down and sorted the good into containers but threw away the bad. So it will be at the close of the age. The angels will come out and separate the evil from the righteous and throw them into the fiery furnace. In that place there will be weeping and gnashing of teeth."

Matthew 13:47-50 English Standard Version

The Parable of the Net

The parable is similar in its teaching to the parable of the wheat and the weeds, and the interpretation has the same phrases concerning the close of the age and the angels' task of separation. Even the words 'throw them into the fiery furnace. In that place there will be weeping and gnashing of teeth' are the same.

The parable of the weeds in the field would be a familiar scene and easily understood by farming folk, and this parable would be crystal clear to his disciples, many of whom were fishermen. The parables both picture the Lord God's final harvest time; the separation of his true and faithful people from others among whom they live.

G. Campbell Morgan sees the whole point of the parable of the net being to re-enforce Jesus' earlier warning, and draw attention yet again to that final separation. 'The main value of the parable, broadly stated, lies in the fact of the separation which is to follow upon the drawing in of the net.'

The detail of the parable
Although the modern mind might like to dwell on the words 'fish of every kind' and think of the good news of the kingdom of heaven, as it is proclaimed gathering people from every social background, intellectual ability and nation throughout the world. True as it is, such thinking does not lie at the heart of the teaching of this parable. This is clearly shown by the Lord's simple division of the good from the bad.

The great variety of things caught in the net is much more likely to be a reflection of what actually happens when fishing in this way. The Greek does not say that the net only gathered fish, and the word for net indicates that it was a trawling net or drag net. Such a net would gather everything in its path as it was drawn through the water. It would gather not only fish but other creatures, weeds and items of rubbish in the water that had been thrown from the shore or a boat.

A puzzling question
If the *kingdom of heaven* is like a drag net, how can it contain people who are good and people who are bad? How can evil people and God's true people be found in heaven, even in the very presence of God? How can the godly and the ungodly be found together anywhere but here on earth?

This has puzzled godly commentators for centuries, and the conclusion is that Jesus was speaking of the kingdom of heaven as it is being gathered here on earth. For this reason, commentators have consistently applied the expression to the visible church on earth, where, from the earliest days, there has always been good and bad mixed.

Matthew Henry comments, 'While the net is in the sea, it is not known what is in it, the fishermen themselves cannot distinguish; but they carefully draw it, and all that is in it, to the shore, for the sake of the good that is in it.' Colourfully applying it to the church, he writes, 'In the visible church there is a deal of trash and rubbish, dirt and weeds and vermin as well as fish.'

The Lord commanded the disciples and those who followed them, to proclaim the gospel widely, to 'every creature'. He called his disciples to be 'fishers of men', and by this parable warned them that they would gather both good and bad into the churches they would found.

The parable of the net prepares us not to be stumbled or offended as we look at the church on earth and find it so imperfect; falling so far short of the ideal expression of kingdom of heaven.

The apostle Paul writes, 'I am not ashamed of the gospel, for it is the power of God to salvation.' And yet, even in the churches the apostle founded, there were 'fish of every kind,' some of whom caused him a great deal of trouble.

J.C. Ryle comments that the parable reflects the true nature of the church as we see it. The parable is a necessary warning, as we can assume that all those gathered into the church are destined for heaven. As Ryle puts it, 'Do we ever hear such teaching? If we do, let us remember "the net"'.

An ongoing work from the very first words

As C.H. Dodd notes, in the ministry of Jesus, and throughout the centuries that have followed, the process of gathering and of separation is going on continuously, '. . . the appeal is made indiscriminately, and yet in the nature of things it is selective . . . this selection is the divine judgment, though men pass it upon themselves by sheer ultimate attitude to the appeal.'

There is this ongoing separation as the good news of the kingdom is proclaimed. Those who hear it either receive it or reject it; take it to heart or ignore it, maybe even scoff at it. But as the parables of the weeds and the net make plain, there is also a final judgment 'on that day' – an ultimate separation of God's true people from others, who had been 'growing in the field' or 'gathered in the net'.

The kingdom of heaven and the visible church on earth
In our day, there are very different understandings of the church:

One view simply equates the visible church on earth with the kingdom of heaven, accepting all among them as truly God's people, destined for a place in heaven. With this understanding, church leaders need simply to keep the church financially sound and the people in their care busy and encouraged. However, the difficulty of this understanding is that it is not in accord with Jesus' teaching about the weedy field, or this parable of the net.

Another view holds that the church on earth should be composed only of true believers and so be able to be equated with the kingdom of heaven. This understanding of the church implies that anyone about whom we entertain doubts must be excluded. The view is, of necessity, somewhat harsh and exclusive. It also creates great difficulties for folk who have grown up among the people of God, talk their language, follow their behaviour and yet are strangers to the One in whom they claim to believe.

A third view, which resonates with this parable, sees the church as a net, gathering people for the Lord, and yet recognising that the people gathered will be a mixture. It then follows that such a church will have the constant responsibility of warning those in their company that there is a day of separation coming, and preparing them for it.

The implications of this parable
If we accept this third understanding of the parable as a picture of the visible church, both those in whose heart a genuine work of God has taken place, and those whose profession of faith will ultimately be found to be only an outward appearance, will be gathered into it.

Within the church, men, women and young people will have all sorts of reasons and motives for being among the people of God. Some will be present for companionship and friendship, some to further their business opportunities, career or marriage prospects, yet others for the pleasure of singing or making music, or to find a role in the local community. Outwardly, all of these good people who have been gathered will appear to be 'wholesome fish,' – but beware.

The parable stands as warning to those whose outward profession is not an inward reality. There is a day coming when secrets of all hearts will be known. In every situation, the test of true faith is obedience. The apostle Paul writes, 'The Lord knows those who are his'; and, 'Let everyone who names the name of the Lord depart from iniquity [ways and life-styles that the Scriptures make plain are displeasing to the Lord God].' The acid test of genuine faith is obedience.

Home-grown church or chapel folk
As the parable would apply to those freshly gathered into the 'church net' in each generation, so it would apply to those born and reared within the 'net', the second and third generation of church or chapel folk. These are people who have grown up surrounded by the outward forms of Christianity, but have yet to discover the underlying reality of the need of true repentance before God and living faith in his anointed Son.

Our churches and chapels are filled with excellent people in exactly this most dangerous state. Until the final separation, there will always be those who only seem like Christian believers among the people of God. To all appearances, they are most wholesome 'fish', and yet know nothing of a close walk with Lord Jesus or the Holy Spirit's life-changing work in their heart and life. They naturally assume that they are members of the kingdom of heaven, and may become eminent leaders in the church. However, on the last day, our Lord would have no choice but to say those terrifying words, 'I never knew you.'

The great responsibility of church leaders
If we accept the implications of this parable, it follows that it is the very serious responsibility of those of us who are church leaders to

pray that the Holy Spirit of God would open eyes and unstop ears, and then clearly to warn all who will hear of this coming day of separation.

As hearers of the word preached:
– We would need to be urged to humbly examine ourselves before God.

– We would need to be given a clear understanding of the commandments and fatherly instructions of the Lord God; an understanding of how he expects people to live in his world, and of the dire and eternal consequences of failing to do so.

– We would need to be given a clear understanding of the gospel call to humble ourselves before God in true repentance for those days and years when we have failed to honour and obey him, turn, and plead for his forgiveness.

– Finally, in order that we might be forgiven, we would need to be given a clear understanding of who Jesus really is, and what it means to have a genuine trusting and obedient faith in 'the Son of God who loved us and gave himself for us.'

A challenge to us all
The parable of the net is a call to examine ourselves before the Lord God, for there is a day coming 'at the close of the age' when there will be a wonderful or terrible final separation between those who are truly the Lord's people and those who only seem to be. It is too easy to be in the net but not, as the apostle Paul puts it, 'in Christ'.

It is salutary to note how often our Lord spoke of the dreadful end of those who fail to humble themselves, accept the gospel and enter the kingdom of heaven 'as a little child'. To help us grasp the seriousness of his warnings, Jesus spoke, as he did in this parable, in terms of everlasting punishment, of fire and of unending torment. Matthew Henry comments that, although not comfortable, 'it is good for us to be often reminded of this awakening, quickening truth.'

A summary of the parable's application then and now
These two parables would prepare Jesus' disciples for what they would find in the fields they were to faithfully sow with good seed, and in the nets of fish they were to gather.

For us, the parables are a great encouragement and a terrible warning. It is an assurance of the Lord God's ultimate justice and love towards those who are truly submitted to him. For those who are not, it is a sharp challenge and warning of a day of separation and final justice.

Heavenly Father, thank you for what is, yet again, a very disturbing and challenging parable spoken by your Son. By your Holy Spirit give us grace to examine ourselves before you, turn and submit to the One who told this parable, and so be certain that we are truly members of the kingdom of heaven.

Questions for personal reflection or discussion

1. 'Fish of every kind', can you think of people in the churches to whom the apostle Paul wrote, who caused the apostle heartache and trouble?
2. Do we naturally assume that all those gathered into the church are destined for heaven? Do we need, as J.C. Ryle puts it, "to remember 'the net'"?
3. Three very different understandings of the church are described, into which does our church or chapel fit most closely? Can the parable of the net help us to clarify our own thinking?
4. In our church, are we often helped and encouraged to humbly examine ourselves before God?
5. Is it comfortable to recognise that until the final separation, there will always be those who only seem like true believers among the people of God?

6. A question for personal reflection. What do we know of yielding ourselves to the Lord God in humble repentance for past failure, and in sincere and obedient faith in the Son of God who loved us and gave himself for us?

References

To proclaim the gospel to 'every creature' – Mark 16:15
He called his disciples to be 'fishers of men' – Luke 5:10, Mark 1:17a

I am not ashamed of the gospel – Romans 1:16
There is also a final judgment 'on that day' – Matthew 7:21-23
Know the One in whom they claim to believe – 2 Timothy 1:12
The Son of God who loved us and gave himself for us – Galatians 2:20
The secrets of our hearts – 1 Samuel 16:7
'The Lord knows those who are his'; and, 'Let everyone who names the name of the Lord depart from iniquity.' – 2 Timothy 2:19
'I never knew you' – Matthew 7:22
'In Christ', as the apostle Paul puts it – 2 Corinthians 5:17
Enter the kingdom of heaven as little child – Matthew 18:2-4
The knowledge of the glory of God in the face of Jesus Christ – 2 Corinthians 4:6

New and Old Treasures

Jesus asked his disciples, "Have you understood all these things?" They said, "Yes."

And he said to them, "Therefore every scribe who has been trained for the kingdom of heaven is like the master of a house, who brings out of his treasure what is new and what is old."

Matthew 13:51-52

Introduction

At first glance, these verses do not seem to fit easily into the flow of Matthew's account and many commentators pass lightly over them. However, they are significant.

William Hendriksen draws attention to the fact that all through his ministry, Jesus was training and preparing his disciples for the great task of teaching others. He will finally commission them, "to make disciples of all nations . . . teaching them to observe all that I have commanded you."

Jesus' question that gave rise to this parable, "Have you understood all these things?" gave the disciples an opportunity to ask the Lord about the parables of growth. The disciples believed they had understood them, and so responded simply, "Yes." Jesus accepted that answer. Having grasped the essence of this part of his teaching, they were able to move on with their training.

The teachers among the Jews in Jesus' day were the 'scribes'. Jesus spoke, of those trained by himself, as 'scribes' of the kingdom. The Greek literally says a 'scribe made a disciple to the kingdom of the heavens.' The disciples were to become teachers or 'scribes' trained in the principles and ways of the kingdom of heaven.

The scribes of Jesus' time were able and diligent scholars, able to read and write and to instruct others. They were well versed in the Old Testament law and were greatly respected. However, the foundation of their training lay in 'the teaching of the elders', the traditions and interpretations that had been laid upon the word of God over many years. Their long and rigorous training was in the teachings of men, rather than in the ways of God, and so they were unable even to recognise the kingdom of heaven and the fulfilment of the prophecies of the Scriptures they had studied – even when it was unfolding before their eyes.

How different were Jesus' 'scribes'. They were trained in the things of the kingdom of heaven, by the King himself, and were being prepared, not to teach human traditions, but to teach the truths of the kingdom of God.

The difference was observed by the rulers, elders and scribes as Peter and John were brought before them on trial. They referred to the disciples as 'ignorant and unlearned men' – which they were if the measure was academic achievement and training in their own traditions – but they took note of the fact that 'they had been with Jesus'. The disciples were students of all that Jesus said and taught them, both in words, and by his example. They were to become familiar with the whole of the God-given Scriptures, and able to see them freshly, without their significance being obscured, or even emptied of meaning, by human teaching.

The difficulties the disciples would face
The question Jesus asked, 'Have you understood these things?' could well, as G. Campbell Morgan suggests, be referring to this whole series of parables. Jesus is asking, 'Have you understood the overall thrust of these parables?' Have you grasped that the kingdom of heaven will come, God's total and absolute rule will be established, yet as you begin to proclaim the gospel of God, calling for repentance and

faith, and then building up disciples, there will be many hindrances, difficulties and challenges?

From the parables Jesus had just taught, it is clear that he was warning them that there would be much to discourage them. There would be hearers with deaf ears and eyes that fail to perceive. There would be those whose faith had very little lasting strength, and those whose hearts would be consumed with the affairs of this world.

The disciples would need great patience. There would be resistance from the world around them which, at heart, is totally opposed to the rule of God, and there would be discouragement for both them and their hearers, because of the cost of faithful discipleship. And behind it all, there would be the fierce resistance of the devil who would sow discouragement, competition, frustration and division, and seek to undermine both their witness, and the rule of God in every way possible.

Masters of the household of God
In this brief parable, Jesus pictures his disciples as 'the master of a house'. A possible translation of the Greek word is 'housemaster', one who carries the responsibility for the well-being of the whole household and has total rule and authority in it. It is the Eastern picture of the absolute ruler of the house, and yet here in the parable, it is a delegated responsibility under the authority of our Lord.

The disciples would never be the owners, but as he taught them elsewhere, they would be chief stewards or managers called to keep order, provide for, and take care of all those in their charge. A chief steward would provide for the household both from fresh produce brought in, and from the stores.

Under their Lord, the disciples were being trained to be the founders and masters of God's household, the people of God, the church.

From his own example, from the teaching and instruction he was giving, and by the enabling of Holy Spirit, Jesus' disciples would be fully-trained and equipped scribes of the kingdom of heaven, well able to take good care of those who would come to faith through their witness. They would be able to hold fast to the Lord's instruction and commands, and also able to apply them to new situations as they arose.

How did the parable of the householder work out in practice?
As the letters in the New Testament clearly show, the disciples proved to be well equipped teachers and managers of our Lord's household. They were also well able to see and explain the fulfilment of the prophecies and promises of the Old Testament. The writings of Matthew and of Paul, and the record of Paul's ministry in the book of Acts, for example, are full of references and convincing arguments showing how the Lord Jesus is the long-promised Messiah, the anointed One, the Christ and the fulfilment of so many prophecies of Scripture.

The application of the parable in our own day – to our 'scribes'
In a similar way to the scribes of Jesus' day, in our own day many of our church leaders and teachers are being thoroughly trained in the traditions of the church, in church history, in philosophy and world affairs, are well-educated and very able. And yet without a vital submission to the Lord Jesus and his teaching and a thorough grounding in them, those of us so trained will make but very poor 'scribes of the kingdom of heaven'.

If the Lord gives us opportunity to teach others, it is our responsibility to keep our own minds filled and fresh, with godly rather than worldly thinking. If we are prayerfully open to the Holy Spirit's teaching, the word of God will challenge our thinking, and the way we are going about things.

The apostle Paul writes, 'All Scripture is breathed out by God and profitable for teaching, for reproof, for correction, and for training in righteousness, that the man of God may be competent, equipped for every good work.' The Scriptures will indeed rebuke, reprove and correct us. That is not always comfortable! Their study will also be part of our ongoing, life-long, 'training in righteousness.' And as there are many old and treasured truths in the word of God, there are also constantly new depths to be plumbed and new insights to be gained.

Matthew Henry commends the scribe of the kingdom of heaven to 'keep his store well stocked' with truths old and new, from the Old and the New Testaments, from his own observations of life and from fresh insights gained from other godly people. With prayer and the Holy Spirit's enlightenment, the study of the Scriptures is a vital and ongoing voyage of discovery. It will keep the teacher or scribe 'well trained in the kingdom of heaven' fresh and able to teach and inspire others.

G. H. Lang notes that scribes like these 'are a perpetual need of the people of God.' Timothy was instructed to appoint as elders only those whose lifestyle was consistent with the gospel and who were 'apt to teach' and willing to 'labour in the word and teaching.'

A central message that includes the old and the new
G. Campbell Morgan considers the essence of 'things old' to be the fact that God is King. It is the call to acknowledge that we are living in God's world, and are commanded to trust, honour and obey him as Lord. Failure to do so carries dire consequences. The call to return to the Lord their God and to submit to his ways was the message, the 'burden', of each of the prophets of the Old Testament and of John the Baptist in the New Testament.

'The new,' entrusted to the disciples and to their successors, is to proclaim the amnesty of God; his gracious and free forgiveness of all who truly confess their failure before him, turn from ungodly ways and believe on his Son who loved us and gave his life for our ransom on the cross. In our Lord's words 'Thus it is written, that the Christ should suffer and on the third day rise from the dead, and that repentance and forgiveness of sins should be proclaimed in his name to all nations, beginning from Jerusalem.'

These two aspects lie at the heart of the message that 'the scribes of the kingdom' are called to teach. We are called to proclaim the Gospel of God and call men and women to turn from God-ignoring, self-centred ways and believe on the Son of God who loved us and laid down his life for or forgiveness. But within that broad definition of our task, there are many aspects old and new which call for exploration and application as appropriate in each situation.

A question for all of us in our day
"Have you understood all these things?" They said to him, "Yes." From the question Jesus asked the disciples, it is clear that he really wanted them to fully grasp the meaning, the significance and personal application of all he had taught. To hear or to read the teaching of the Lord Jesus is one thing. It is quite another to be willing to allow his teaching to direct our hearts and our wills, and determine to put his warnings, promises and teaching into practice in our daily lives.

A great many of those who heard our Lord's parables fell far short of such 'understanding'. They enjoyed listening, but their way of thinking and living remained untouched. Beware, for exactly the same is happening in our day. So many attend our places of worship, enjoy meeting and singing together, but so few grow in understanding or in 'grace and knowledge of our Lord and Saviour Jesus Christ,' as the apostle Peter put it.

Life abundant, lived for the glory of God
As William Barclay notes, being trained as a 'scribe of the kingdom' in no way shrank or made lesser men of those who Jesus called. It enabled those he trained to use all the natural strengths, skills, learning and experience they had previously gained to live for the glory of God, for the furtherance of the kingdom of heaven and for the welfare of those entrusted to their care.

Peter, for example, was by nature a leader and the first to speak. Once he and the others were filled with the Holy Spirit on the Day of

Pentecost, Peter was on his feet and able to boldly explain what had happened and to proclaim the gospel.

With his understanding now enlightened by his encounter with the Lord Jesus on the road to Damascus, the apostle Paul was able to employ all his training as a Pharisee, no longer to attack the Gospel, but to proclaim and defend it.

As that principle applied to the Apostles, so it also applies to all those the Lord calls today. He sets free all our God-given powers, experiences and skills to be used for the glory of his name and the extension of his kingdom. It is our responsibility to go on actively discovering how this new, humble, grateful and willingly obedient relationship with the Father and his Son works itself out in practical trust and obedience, in the age in which we live, in our own personal lives, in our society and in our national arrangements and laws.

Heavenly Father, thank you for this parable, brief as it is. We ask that you would enable us to use the opportunities you give to us, whether they are great or small, to live for the glory of your name and the furtherance of your kingdom.

Questions for reflection or discussion

1. The disciples were students of all Jesus said and taught them in words, and by his example. How can we help and stir one another to be like those first disciples?
2. Is it true that, although there are many people who are able and willing to speak in our churches, yet without a vital submission to the Lord Jesus and his teaching and a thorough grounding in them, they – or we – 'will make but very poor 'scribes' of the kingdom of heaven'?

3. With the enlightenment of the Holy Spirit, delight in the study of the Scriptures is a vital and ongoing voyage of discovery. As that applies to our 'scribes' does it apply to each one of us?

4. 'Thus it is written, that the Christ should suffer and on the third day rise from the dead, and that repentance and forgiveness of sins should be proclaimed in his name to all nations, beginning from Jerusalem.' Is this being proclaimed as widely as it could be? What part can we play?

5. Are we really willing to allow Jesus' teaching to direct our will, and determine to put his commands and teaching into practice in our day by day living?

6. To what extent are we faithfully using all our experiences and skills for the glory of his name and the extension of his kingdom? How can we help one another?

References

To make disciples of all nations – Matthew 28:19-20
They had been with Jesus – Acts 4:13
Managers set over the household – Luke 12:42-43 and Matthew 24:45
Profitable for teaching, for reproof, for correction, and for training – 2 Timothy 3:16-17.
Apt to teach – 1 Timothy 3:2
Willing to labour in the word and teaching – 1 Timothy 5:17
Repentance and forgiveness of sins should be proclaimed in his name to all nations, beginning from Jerusalem – Luke 24:46-47
Grace and knowledge our Lord and Saviour Jesus Christ – 2Peter3:18

The Lost Sheep

At that time the disciples came to Jesus, saying, "Who is the greatest in the kingdom of heaven?" And calling to him a child, he put him in the midst of them and said, "Truly, I say to you unless you turn and become as little children, you will never enter the kingdom of heaven. Whoever humbles himself like this child is the greatest in the kingdom of heaven.

"Whoever receives one such child in my name receives me, but whoever causes one of these who believe in me to sin, it would be better for him to have a great millstone fastened round his neck and to be drowned in the depth of the sea.

"Woe to the world for temptations to sin! For it is necessary that temptations come, but woe to the one by whom the temptation comes! And if your hand or your foot causes you to sin, cut it off and throw it away. It is better for you to enter life crippled or lame than with two hands or two feet be thrown into the eternal fire. And if your eye causes you to sin, tear it out and throw it away. It is better for you to enter life with one eye than with two eyes to be thrown into the hell of fire.

"See that you do not despise one of these little ones; for I tell you that in heaven their angels always see the face of my Father who is in heaven. What do you think? If a man has a hundred sheep and one of them has gone astray, does he not leave the ninety-nine on the mountains and go in search of the one that went astray? So it is not the will of my Father who is in heaven that one of these little ones should perish."

Matthew 18:1-14 English Standard Version

Now the tax collectors and sinners were all drawing near to hear him. And the Pharisees and the scribes grumbled, saying, "This man receives sinners and eats with them." So he told them this parable: "What man of you, having a hundred sheep, if he has lost one of them, does not leave the ninety-nine in the open country, and go after the one that is lost, until he finds it? And when he has found it, he lays it on his shoulders, rejoicing. And when he comes home, he calls together his friends and his neighbours, saying to them, 'Rejoice with me, for I have found my sheep that was lost.' Just so, I tell you, there will be more joy in heaven over one sinner who repents than over ninety-nine righteous persons who need no repentance'.

Luke 15:1-7 English Standard Version

The Lost Sheep

This brief parable in Matthew's Gospel is easily overlooked. However, as well as its immediate application, it sheds a clear light on the nature of the love and care of the Lord God for his people, and on who the Lord Jesus truly is, and what he came to do. The parable is a window through which we can see one of the great themes of Scripture.

The setting of the parable
The parable of the shepherd seeking his lost or straying sheep is found in the Gospels of Matthew and of Luke. The setting is different, but in each case the point of the parable was to show that, like a true shepherd, the Lord Jesus takes great care of his flock. Not one must be neglected, discounted, left to stray or be lost.

A parable for the disciples
On the occasion recorded by Matthew, the parable is addressed to the disciples who had been arguing among themselves who would be the greatest among them in Jesus' forthcoming kingdom.

The parallel passages in Mark and Luke throw further light on their debate and on Jesus' response to it:

Mark writes, 'And they came to Capernaum. And when he was in the house he asked them, "What were you discussing on the way?" But they kept silent, for they had argued with one another about who was the greatest. And he sat down and called the twelve. And he said to them, "If anyone would be first, he must be last of all and servant of all." And he took a child and put him in the midst of them, and taking him in his arms, he said to them, "Whoever receives one such child in my name receives me, and whoever receives me, receives not me but him who sent me." Mark 9:33-37

Luke records, 'An argument arose among them as to which of them was the greatest. But Jesus, knowing the reasoning of their hearts, took a child and put him by his side and said to them, "Whoever receives this child in my name receives me, and whoever receives me receives him who sent me. For he who is least among all of you is the one who is great."' Luke 9:46-48

Jesus turned the self-centred and self-seeking thinking of the disciples on its head by putting before them a young child. The parable of the lost sheep was given to teach the disciples that they were not to be preoccupied with worldly matters and career prospects, or who could secure the best places in our Lord's future government and so be the greatest. They were to spend their lives as faithful shepherds; searching for, bringing home, encouraging and building up the lost, neglected and hurting people of God. It was the pattern the Lord himself set as he taught the common people, cared for the sick and suffering, the poor and the lost, the fallen and the little child he placed among them.

By his teaching, his example and by this parable, Jesus made plain to the disciples that they were not to follow the self-seeking ways of the world, or of the scribes and Pharisees, but to learn from him and follow his pattern of genuine care for every one of God's people.

Speaking with the disciples, Jesus said, "See that you do not despise one of these little ones . . . What do you think? If a man has a hundred sheep and one of them has gone astray, does he not leave the ninety-nine on the mountains and go in search of the one that went astray? So it is not the will of my Father who is in heaven that one of these little ones should perish."

Who are these 'little ones'? Children and young people, certainly, for Jesus placed a young child before the disciples. However, it is clear from the record of our Lord's ministry that he cared all God's people – full-grown men and women, rich and poor, old and young, those held in honour and those excluded, cast out and despised, sick, suffering, broken or fallen, as well as children. These are all 'the sheep' of his 'fold.'

For this same reason Jesus reprimanded the disciples when they tried to deter the ordinary people who were bringing their little ones to him for his blessing.

After his resurrection, Jesus commissioned the apostles to 'go into all the world and preach the gospel,' and to 'make disciples of all nations.' The parable of the lost sheep challenged them not to be concerned with their own career, status and standing, but to be concerned for the spiritual and the physical wellbeing of all the Lord's people. They were to learn from Jesus' own example and be faithful, patient, and compassionate shepherds of all those to whom he sent them, and to all those people he brought across their path.

That the disciples learned the lesson is plainly to be seen in the early chapters of the book of Acts. Peter, filled with the Holy Spirit, grasped the God-given opportunity, on the Day of Pentecost, to preach the gospel and call his fellow Jews to repent before God, and he, and his fellow apostles, led and taught the newly baptized believers. A few days later, he and John had compassion on the lame man who was begging for money at the gate of the temple. In the name of the Lord Jesus they healed him, and again Peter was given opportunity to preach the Gospel to great effect.

As the parable was a challenge to the disciples in their day, so it is an on-going challenge for ministers and people alike in our day.

A parable for the Pharisees
On the separate occasion recorded by Luke, the parable was addressed to the scribes and Pharisees in response to their murmuring, and confirming one another in their rejection of Jesus as the long awaited Messiah. The reason why they murmured and rejected him was because he was mixing, and even eating, with tax gatherers and sinners. The parable was one of a series of parables making clear to the scribes and Pharisees why he was mixing with and caring for such people.

The religious leaders were very concerned to preserve their own position and their own religious status and were consumed with keeping themselves, according to their traditions, 'uncontaminated' by the world, and so in their eyes 'acceptable to God'. To achieve this they had to be ritually clean, and so they kept themselves separate. They even came to despise the very people for whom they were called to care. They despised the common people and those who failed to keep their traditions and, in common with the thinking of the age, they had no concern for the fallen, for women, children or those of any other race.

The people with whom Jesus was mixing were the people of God who, for lack of true teaching and due care had strayed, and perhaps strayed far. However, in the eyes of the Pharisees, they were unrighteous, unclean and to be disregarded as 'people of no value' – thieving, traitorous, tax collectors for the Roman conquerors, or fallen 'sinners' in some other way.

By the series of parables, Jesus was showing the scribes and Pharisees, as God's under-shepherds, their own mistaken self-righteousness and, as a result of it, their failure to care for God's people, including such 'lost and straying sheep'.

The parable stands as a warning to us as, in our day too, we can easily judge by the outward circumstances of those the Lord brings across our path, and fail to help them – but the Lord God looks on the heart.

The shepherd and his sheep – a key parable

The two different settings of the parable of the shepherd and the straying sheep are of great value, because at as well as their immediate application, our Lord unfolds the profound reason why he, the Son of God, laid aside the glory of heaven and came among us.

Speaking with the disciples, and with the scribes and Pharisees, was the Son of God, Emmanuel, God among his people, seeking and rescuing his precious but lost sheep.

The parable is a key to understanding the whole purpose of the Lord God in sending his Son into this world. He came in order to fulfil the many prophecies, found throughout the Psalms and the Prophets, that the Lord God would come among his people to rescue his straying, lost and neglected sheep.

The united testimony of the Scriptures

The picture of the Lord God as the shepherd of his people is one of the great themes of the Scriptures. From the Psalms of David, himself a shepherd looking after his father's flock, through the writings of the Prophets and on into the New Testament.

In Psalm 23 King David sings personally, 'The Lord is my shepherd; I shall not want . . .' Many of the other Psalms reflect the fact that the Lord God's people are his sheep, so Psalm 100 reads, 'It is he who made us, and we are his people, and the sheep of his pasture.'

The prophet Isaiah writes, 'Behold the Lord God comes with might ... He will tend his flock like a shepherd, he will gather the lambs in his arms; and carry them in his bosom, and gently lead those who are with young.'

Jeremiah warns, "Woe to the shepherds who destroy and scatter the sheep of my pasture!" declares the Lord. Therefore thus says the Lord, the God of Israel, concerning the shepherds who care for my people: "You have scattered my flock and have driven them away, and you have not attended to them.

"Behold I will attend to you for your evil deeds, declares the Lord. Then I will gather the remnant of my flock out of the countries where I have driven them, and I will bring them back to their fold, and they shall be fruitful and multiply. I will set shepherds over them who will care for them, and they shall fear no more, nor be dismayed, neither shall any be missing, declares the Lord.

"Behold the days are coming, declares the Lord, when I will raise up for David a righteous Branch, and he shall reign as king and deal wisely, and shall execute justice and righteousness in the land. In his days Judah will be saved, and Israel will dwell securely. And this is the name by which he will be called: 'The Lord is our righteousness.'"

The prophet Ezekiel proclaimed that the Lord himself, under the figure of David the faithful shepherd king, would come among the people of Israel to rescue his neglected people, his sheep. 'Son of man, prophesy against the shepherds of Israel; prophesy, and say to them, even to the shepherds, Thus says the Lord God; Ah, shepherds of Israel who have been feeding yourselves! Should not a shepherd feed the sheep? . . . I myself will be the shepherd of my sheep, and I myself will make them lie down, declares the Lord God. I will seek the lost, and will bring back the strayed, and will bind up the injured, and I will strengthen the weak . . .' 'And I will set up over them one shepherd, my servant David, and he shall feed them: he shall feed them and be their shepherd. And I, the Lord, will be their God, and my servant David shall be prince among them. I am the Lord; I have spoken.'

The prince and shepherd of God's people
For those with eyes to see, it is clear from the Gospels that these prophecies are fulfilled in the One addressed throughout his ministry

by such titles as the 'Son of David', the 'Holy One of God', the 'Son of God', and 'the King who comes in the name of the Lord'.

Throughout the New Testament the reality of the Lord God as the shepherd of his people takes flesh and blood in the person of the Son of God, the Lord Jesus, the 'great shepherd of the sheep'.

The Lord God has entrusted the responsibility of being the prince and shepherd of his people to his anointed Son, the Lord Jesus, to whom he has given all authority.

The Lord Jesus came, as he said of himself, 'to seek and to save that which was lost.' Not one must be lost, from the humblest child to the most deeply fallen sinner.

What did Jesus say of himself as shepherd of God's people?
Mark records that on one occasion Jesus said to the apostles, '"Come away by yourselves to a desolate place [a quiet and sparsely populated place] and rest a while." For many were coming and going, and they had no leisure even to eat. And they went away in the boat to a desolate place by themselves. Now many saw them going and recognised them, and they ran there on foot from all the towns and got there ahead of them. When Jesus went ashore he saw a great crowd, and he had compassion on them, because they were like sheep without a shepherd. And he began to teach them many things.'

In a similar way, Matthew records, 'And Jesus went throughout all the cities and villages, teaching in their synagogues and proclaiming the gospel of the kingdom and healing every disease and every affliction. When he saw the crowds, he had compassion on them, because they were like sheep without a shepherd. Then he said to his disciples, "The harvest is plentiful, but the labourers are few, therefore pray earnestly to the Lord of the harvest to send out labourers into his harvest."

The apostle John records Jesus teaching, 'The sheep hear [the shepherd's] voice, and he calls his own sheep by name and leads them out.

When he has brought out all his own, he goes before them, and the sheep follow him, for they know his voice. A stranger they will not follow, but they will flee from him, for they do not know the voice of strangers . . . Jesus said to them, "Truly, truly, I say to you, I am the door of the sheep. . . If anyone enters by me, he will be saved and go in and out and find pasture. . . I am the good shepherd. The good shepherd lays down his life for the sheep. . . I know my own and my own know me, just as the Father knows me and I know the Father, and I lay down my life for the sheep. And I have other sheep that are not of this fold. I must bring them also, and they will listen to my voice. So there will be one flock and one shepherd.'"

Approaching his arrest in the garden of Gethsemane, Jesus warned the disciples, "You will all fall away because of me this night. For it is written, 'I will strike the shepherd and the sheep of the flock will be scattered.'"

After the resurrection, as our Jesus restored Peter after he had denied his Lord three times, Jesus specifically charged him to 'feed my sheep' and to 'tend my lambs.'

The great range of God's people our Lord was shepherding
Jesus cared about the great crowds of ordinary people who were not being taught faithfully, and so when he taught them, they were eager to hear him. They 'knew his voice', for he taught them with all the authority of the word of God. Not with the current opinions of the time, or, as the scribes and Pharisees did, with their own 'time-honoured traditions'.

The Gospel writers also make plain that our Lord spent a great deal of time and trouble explaining the ways of God to God's 'less than faithful' under-shepherds, the scribes and Pharisees. Sometimes this took place openly in his public teaching as they challenged him, at other times it was over a meal where 'they watched him', examining his teaching and putting him in testing situations. An example of this would be the meal described in Luke chapter 14, where Jesus was confronted with a man with dropsy in order to see if he would heal him on the Sabbath day. On each occasion he was showing the Pharisees who he was and why he was caring for such people, and showing them in what ways they were falling short before God.

The Lord Jesus also cared for despised individual 'sinners' like the prostitute who washed his feet with her tears. And he took trouble with hated men like Matthew and Zacchaeus, who were gathering taxes for the Romans.

Although he came primarily to gather the lost sheep of the house of Israel, Jesus did not reject the cries of believing people from other nations. He healed the Roman centurion's servant with a word, and a Samaritan leper. When Jesus was in the district of Tyre and Sidon a local woman came crying to him to heal her daughter, "Have mercy on me, O Lord, Son of David . . ." 'He answered, "I was sent only to the lost sheep of the house of Israel." But she persisted, and came and knelt before him, saying, "Lord help me." . . . Then Jesus answered her, "O woman, great is your faith! Be it done for you as you desire." And her daughter was healed instantly.'

After Jesus had chosen the twelve, who he named apostles, he sent them out, saying, "Go nowhere among the Gentiles and enter no town of the Samaritans, but go rather to the lost sheep of the house of Israel."

As a true shepherd, Jesus not only had compassion on the humble and meek but also on those in high position. He had compassion on the ruler of the synagogue whose little daughter was on the point of death. Yet he also had compassion on the woman, greatly distressed by her continued flow of blood, as she 'interrupted him' on his way to the ruler's house.

The Son of God, the great shepherd of Israel, was gathering into God's fold all those in whom God had sown seeds of faith; this included the poor, the outcasts and those rejected by the religious leaders as 'of no value' or ritually unclean.

Further references to the Lord Jesus as shepherd
In the great cry of praise, the writer to the letter to the Hebrews describes Jesus as 'the great shepherd of the sheep'. 'Now may the God of peace who brought again from the dead our Lord Jesus, the great shepherd of the sheep, by the blood of the eternal covenant, equip you with everything good that you may do his will, working in us that which pleasing in his sight, through Jesus Christ, to whom be glory for ever and ever. Amen.'

The apostle Peter, writing to believers scattered in exile, says, 'By his wounds you have been healed. For you were straying like sheep, but have now returned to the shepherd and overseer of your souls.' And, after setting out the godly pattern of leadership to the elders of the church, he refers to the Lord Jesus as the 'chief shepherd', saying, 'And when the chief shepherd appears, you will receive the unfading crown of glory.'

A challenge to this generation
For ourselves in our day, each of us is called to do nothing to hinder and to do all we can to further God's great purpose of gathering his precious, chosen people into his fold.

Heavenly Father, thank you for this short parable, easily overlooked in Matthew's Gospel, and yet so significant to our understanding of your sending your one and only Son into this world as the prince and shepherd of your people.

By your Holy Spirit enable us to be faithful to your calling on our lives in our generation. We pray for our fellow believers and church leaders, that we may learn from the parable to beware of both the self-seeking attitude of the disciples and of the self-satisfied, self-righteous and self-protecting ways of the scribes and Pharisees of our Lord's day. And we pray that you would awaken and stir us to play our part in your great purpose of gathering your people into your fold.

Questions for reflection or discussion

1. Speaking with the disciples, what were the characteristics Jesus described of those who are truly great in the kingdom of heaven?

2. Does Jesus' teaching on greatness touch our own thinking and way of going about things?

3. Like both the Pharisees and the disciples at that time, can we, too, be too busy about our own affairs and too concerned about our own status to care for those the Lord brings across our path?

4. Can we, too, be deflected by the outward circumstances of someone and so fail to hear the quiet cry and longing of their heart to be right with God, and a member of the kingdom of heaven?

5. It is easy to pass over this parable in Matthew's Gospel, especially as it features so much more prominently in Luke. Why is it such a key parable?

6. How did this parable challenge the disciples, and in what ways can it challenge us to be involved as his under-shepherds and present day witnesses to his love and his mercy?

References

And they came to Capernaum – Mark 9:33-37
An argument arose among – Luke 9:46-48
Go into all the world and preach the Gospel – Mark 16:15
Make disciples of all nations – Matthew 28:19
The disciples regarded as uneducated – Acts 2:14-24 and 3:1-4:4
The parable addressed to the Pharisees – Luke 15:1-7
The Lord God looks on the heart – 1 Samuel 16:7
The Lord is my shepherd – Psalm 23
The sheep of your pasture – Psalms 79:13, 95:7 and 100:3
He will tend his flock like a shepherd – Isaiah 40:10-11
Woe to the shepherds who . . . scatter the sheep – Jeremiah 23:1-6
I will be the shepherd of my sheep – Ezekiel 34:11-16, 23-24

THE LOST SHEEP · 83

Son of David – Luke 18:35-38
Holy One of God – Mark 1:23-24
Son of God – Matthew 8:28-29 and John 1:34
The King who comes in the name of the Lord – Luke 19:38
The great shepherd of the sheep – Hebrews 13:20 -21
With authority – Matthew 7:28-29, and, all authority – Matthew 28:18
To seek and to save the lost – Luke 19:10
Like sheep without a shepherd – Mark 6:31-34
The harvest is plentiful, but the labourers are few – Luke 10:2
Jesus the shepherd of his sheep – John 10:2-16
The sheep hear [the shepherd's] voice – John 10:3-16
I will strike . . . and the sheep will be scattered – Matthew 26:31
Feed my sheep: John 21:15-17
The meal described in Luke chapter 14 – Luke 14:1-6
Matthew – Matthew 9:9-13
Zacchaeus – Luke 19:1-10
He healed the Centurion's servant with a word - Luke 7:2-10
He healed a Samaritan leper – Luke 17:11-19
Tyre and Sidon woman's daughter – Matthew 15:21-28
The lost sheep of the house of Israel – Matthew 10:5
The ruler of the synagogue, and the woman – Luke 8:40-56
The great shepherd of the sheep – Hebrews 13:20 -21
The shepherd and overseer of your souls – 1 Peter 2:25
When the chief shepherd appears – 1 Peter 5:4

Footnote, *additional references to the Lord God as the 'Shepherd of his People'*

Isaiah 53:6, 'All we like sheep have gone astray; we have turned every one to his own way; and the Lord has laid on him the iniquity of us all.'

Jeremiah 31 v. 10, "Hear the word of the Lord, O nations, and declare it in the coastlands far away; say, 'He who scattered Israel will gather him, and will keep him as a shepherd keeps his flock.'

Zechariah 13 v. 7 speaks of the shepherd being struck and the sheep scattered, "Awake, O sword against my shepherd, against the man who stands next to me," declares the Lord of hosts. "Strike the shepherd, and the sheep will be scattered . . ." Jesus quoted this prophecy as he warned the disciples of his forthcoming arrest, trial and crucifixion. (Matthew 26:31)

The Unmerciful Servant

Then Peter came up and said to him, "Lord, how often will my brother sin against me, and I forgive him? As many as seven times?" Jesus said to him, "I do not say to you seven times, but seventy times seven.

Therefore, the kingdom of heaven may be compared to a king who wished to settle accounts with his servants. When he began to settle, one was brought to him who owed him ten thousand talents. And since he could not pay, his master ordered him to be sold, with his wife and children and all that he had, and payment to be made. So the servant fell on his knees, imploring him, 'Have patience with me, and I will pay you everything.' And out of pity for him, the master of that servant released him and forgave him the debt.

But when that same servant went out, he found one of his fellow servants who owed him a hundred denarii, and seizing him, he began to choke him, saying, 'Pay what you owe.' So his fellow servant fell down and pleaded with him, 'Have patience with me, and I will pay you.' He refused and went and put him in prison until he should pay the debt. When his fellow servants saw what had taken place, they were greatly distressed, and they went and reported to their master all that had taken place.

Then his master summoned him and said to him, 'You wicked servant! I forgave you all that debt because you pleaded with me. And should not you have had mercy on your fellow servant, as I had mercy on you?' And in anger his master delivered him to the jailers, until he should pay all his debt. So also will my heavenly Father do to every one of you, if you do not forgive your brother from your heart."

                        Matthew 18:21-35 English Standard Version

The Unmerciful Servant

The setting of the parable
Jesus had just been teaching his disciples about dealing with fellow believers who had fallen, even, should it prove necessary, to the extent of the excluding of them from the fellowship of believers. The aim was to help fallen disciples to see the gravity of their fault and to stir them to turn from it, and make possible their forgiveness and restoration to the fellowship.

It was with this teaching in mind that Peter asked the Lord a question about personal forgiveness, "Lord, how often will my brother sin against me, and I forgive him? As many as seven times?" Peter was being very generous. Over the years, the Pharisees had pondered this and had decided that three times and then no more, was enough. So Peter must have considered he was being exceedingly generous in offering to forgive more than twice that number of times.

However, there was a problem with Peter's question. It assumed that there was a point when one should feel no sympathy or need to forgive any more. The offending person had forfeited any hope of forgiveness.

The Lord Jesus rejected this rule-making and rule-keeping way of thinking – which was typical of the scribes and Pharisees – and, by way of this parable, taught his disciples a lesson that very much goes against our natural human reaction to any slur, offence, deception, loss of money, or challenge to our good name or status. Jesus taught his disciples – and all those of us who have come to believe through their testimony – to be prepared to offer personal forgiveness without any limit.

The parable itself
'Therefore, the kingdom of heaven may be compared to a king who wished to settle accounts with his servants. When he began to settle, one was brought to him who owed him ten thousand talents. And since

he could not pay, his master ordered him to be sold, with his wife and children and all that he had, and payment to be made.'

Arthur Carr comments that the parable pictures an Eastern Court with an absolute sovereign ruler. Even the most high-ranking of his officials are his 'slaves' accountable to him – as Joseph was in Egypt, even though he was first minister under Pharaoh, and as Daniel was under King Darius, who planned to set him over the whole kingdom 'because an excellent spirit was in him.'

The vastness of the debt the servant owed
In the parable, it is clear that provincial governors, chief tax collectors and other high officials were summoned to give account of their administrations. The servant described owed more than a typical king's total wealth! Ten thousand talents is a vast sum. It is on record that even Solomon's magnificent, gold-covered temple cost little more than three thousand talents.

Following the standard practice of that day, the king 'ordered him to be sold, with his wife and children and all that he had, and payment to be made.' The servant was a bankrupt debtor fit only to be sold as a bond slave to pull the oar in a galley or grind grain in a prison house.

The servant fell on his knees, imploring him, 'Have patience with me, and I will pay you everything.' What hope had he really got of repaying such a debt? Harold Lindsell calculated that for the servant to repay his debt from the wages of a working man would take about 150,000 years. It would be totally impossible.

Yet 'out of pity for him, the master of that servant released him and forgave him the debt.' This was unheard of mercy. It was far beyond the realms of any just settlement, and it was granted at great cost to the king in lost revenue. It was mercy without limit.

The smallness of the debt the servant was owed by his fellow servant
However, the servant, on leaving his master's presence, far from being overwhelmed by relief, and the mercy his master had shown him, and

reflecting that generosity. '. . . found one of his fellow servants who owed him a hundred denarii, and seizing him, he began to choke him, saying, 'Pay what you owe.' So his fellow servant fell down and pleaded with him, 'Have patience with me, and I will pay you.'

Despite his own very recent forgiveness, he took him by the throat. Even though his fellow servant only asked for patience and time to repay the debt, he would have none of it.

Calculating it in the same way as the vast debt he had just been forgiven, his fellow servant owed him approximately three month's wages. But he was not willing to hear the cries for mercy or give his fellow servant time to repay. 'He refused and went and put him in prison until he should pay the debt.'

To picture the immensity of the debt the first servant owed to his master and compare it with the smallness of his fellow servant's debt, William Barclay comments that the fellow servant could repay his debt from a single bag of coins. However, to pay the debt the forgiven servant owed to his master would take 500,000 bags – an army of men carrying sacks of coins!

The king's reaction

'When his fellow servants saw what had taken place, they were greatly distressed, and they went and reported to their master all that had taken place. Then his master summoned him and said to him, 'You wicked servant! I forgave you all that debt because you pleaded with me. And should not you have had mercy on your fellow servant, as I had mercy on you?' And in anger his master delivered him to the jailers, until he should pay all his debt.'

The king was rightly furious, and by his behaviour towards his fellow servant, the unforgiving servant forfeited his own forgiveness. Matthew Henry comments, '. . . see how the punishment answers the sin; he that would not forgive shall not be forgiven.'

The Lord Jesus concluded, 'So also will my heavenly Father do to every one of you, if you do not forgive your brother from your heart.'

The vivid picture of the forgiven servant's lack of mercy and patience toward his fellow servant would have been absolutely shocking to our Lord's first hearers. And, as Richard Trench comments, it is difficult imagine how any amount of teaching and instruction could convey this truth with all the force and conviction of this parable.

The parable's relevance to believers today

The greatness of the debt we owe

The servant had no hope of repaying the debt he owed to the king, yet like a drowning man clutching at a straw, he fancied he could repay it all. How strongly our instinct for self preservation and our pride clings!

By human nature, we live in God's world as if he did not exist and hardly notice our own 'minor imperfections' – or even our major ones. We tend to compare ourselves with 'worse sinners' and so look favourably on ourselves.

However, by this parable Jesus displayed the nature of our debt before Almighty God in its true proportion. As his creatures, we have failed to obey even the Lord God's most basic command to live in a way that brings honour to his name: to honour, love and obey him.

Confronted by the truth of our failure before the Lord God, we, like the servant, will grasp at anything that might give us hope of excusing ourselves; we may blame our genes, our circumstances or the pressures and enticements of the world around us. Only when these are seen to be empty and fail to help us, will we bend the knee, humble ourselves and plead for mercy.

We may ignore our debt before our Maker for decades, but the stoutest heart will fail when God sets our sins before us. As Archbishop Trench puts it, when the Lord God alarms our conscience by the prospect of imminent death 'so that there is not a step between us and it' and sets our failures before us, we find 'our trespasses are more than the hairs on our head.'

Before the overwhelming glory, purity and holiness of God, we are all of us totally lost and undone. Like the servant before his king, our only hope lies with the totally unearned mercy and grace of God.

The king's forgiveness of the servant is a picture of pure grace, reflecting the infinite greatness of the Lord God's willingness to forgive us his fallen creatures when we truly turn to him, guilty and empty-handed, and beg for his mercy.

Our obligation to forgive those around us
Writing about the parable, Arthur Carr comments, 'The chief lesson is the example of the divine spirit of forgiveness in the act of the king. This is the example the pardoned slave should have followed' – and the example every forgiven disciple of Christ is called to follow.

Yet, blinded by our pride and self esteem, we have so little idea of the immensity of the Lord God's love, kindness and mercy towards us – or of our duty to reflect that kindness and mercy to those around us.

Having ourselves pleaded for mercy, and been granted great and free forgiveness, we have bound ourselves to reflect our heavenly Father's treatment of us in our dealings with our fellow human beings.

Followers of our Lord are called cultivate a consistent, godly habit of a forgiving spirit; putting up with much, bearing with much, and very generous with forgiveness. Our aim should be to promote harmony and the good of the whole community and to avoid awakening the 'old nature' of strife, revenge and retaliation – within ourselves or within other people.

How much difficulty and division is caused when that 'old nature' rears its head and we take great offence at some 'perceived injustice' or infringement of what we see as one of 'our rights'.

On this point, Matthew Henry warns that we must learn to forgive those who offend us from the heart and not just with our mouth – as we secretly plan our revenge! If we do not forgive them from the heart, we are putting into question our own profession of faith, for if we have truly believed, repented and been forgiven, it will show in our treatment of the sometimes difficult people in the world around us.

Keeping a level head
Peter had just asked at what point he could justly withhold forgiveness from a 'brother'. So his question was about personal forgiveness of the rubs and bumps and personal offences of everyday life.

J. C. Ryle comments that we should be very grateful to the Lord for showing disciples how to respond when ill-treated, for in this fallen world, we will be! The Lord Jesus lays down as a general rule that we should 'forgive to the uttermost' This does not mean that we are to allow people to steal our property or assault us with impunity and so encourage them to take advantage of us. But it does mean that we are to study a general spirit of mercy and forgiveness towards those around us.

John Calvin notes that our Lord is not calling his disciples to abandon common sense or discernment. It is not for us to pass lightly over or make light of what the Lord God has declared is hateful in his sight. No one can forgive theft, defrauding, rape or murder but God alone.

If we are victims of such things, it is not for us to offer hasty words of forgiveness. The matter needs to be put in the hands of those whose task it is to maintain the law, or the offender will be encouraged to take advantage of us, and of others, and commit further crimes. But it is for us to bear no malice, and to do all that is in our power to encourage those who are guilty to repent before God and live a godly life in future.

Such personal forgiveness was often taught by the Lord Jesus
Again and again Jesus repeats this teaching of on-going, godlike forgiveness, actively urging disciples to make it a constant practice to forgive, until it becomes habitual and a part of godly character.

For example, our Lord had already taught the Lord's Prayer with the phrase, 'forgive us our trespasses as we forgive those who trespass against us,' or as it is in the English Standard Version, reflecting the Greek, ''. . . and forgive us our debts as we have forgiven our debtors.'

After concluding that pattern prayer, the Lord added, 'For if you forgive others their trespasses, your heavenly Father will also forgive you, but if you do not forgive others their trespasses, neither will your Father forgive your trespasses.'

It is not that, by being forgiving of others, we can earn the Lord God's forgiveness of our failures before him. But, like the servant in the parable, we can forfeit any hope of our own forgiveness, if we refuse to forgive others.

Our Lord has made it painfully clear, that the one thing God will not forgive is an unforgiving heart.

In Luke 17:3-4, we read our Lord saying, "Pay attention to yourselves! If your brother sins, rebuke him, and if he repents, forgive him, and if he sins against you seven times in a day, and turns to you seven times, saying, 'I repent', you must forgive him."

Like a young child singing out, "Sorry!" as if the word would cure all wrongdoing; it is rather too easy to just say, 'I repent' – it costs us nothing. True repentance before the Lord God has consequences, it is always costly. It involves an ongoing turning away from wrong doing, and every effort made to put right the wrongs done.

As John the Baptist proclaimed his message of repentance, he called on his hearers to show their sincerity by demonstrating 'fruits in keeping with repentance.' With real repentance and forgiveness there will be deeply grateful heart and clear evidence. As Jesus taught in this parable, a key piece of evidence will be a forgiving disposition towards those around us.

In conclusion
By way of this parable, our Lord spells out two powerful motives to help us. Firstly, to constantly reflect on just how much the Lord God has forgiven us, and the great cost of that forgiveness. Secondly, to bear in mind our Lord's dreadful warning as he concluded this parable – lest, like the servant in the parable, by our refusal to forgive others, we forfeit the Lord God's forgiveness of ourselves.

As the parable makes plain, having begged for the forgiveness of Almighty God and in mercy been given it, we bind ourselves to being kind, merciful, patient and forgiving to those around us. In truth, hard as it is, such a willingness to forgive 'from the heart' is the hallmark of the true believer.

Heavenly Father, we thank you for your mercy and forgiveness. We ask you to remind us of this parable when our natural human unwillingness to forgive others rears its ugly head. May we learn to be as patient, generous, kind and forgiving of others as you have been of us.

Questions for reflection or group discussion

1. 'Jesus had just been teaching his disciples about dealing with fellow believers who had fallen, even – should it prove necessary, to the extent of the excluding of them from the fellowship of believers. The aim was to help fallen disciples to see the gravity of their fault and to stir them to turn from it, and make possible their forgiveness and restoration to the fellowship.' – Do we, and should we, still discipline believers who have badly fallen like this?

2. 'There was a problem with Peter's question. It assumed that there was a point at which forgiveness should no more be offered, and that beyond that point one should feel no sympathy or obligation to forgive. The offending person had forfeited any hope of forgiveness.'

– "That's the fourth time you've done that!" Can we be guilty thinking like that, and of counting up offences in that way?

4. 'The Lord Jesus rejected this rule-making and rule-keeping thinking – which was typical of the scribes and Pharisees – and, by way of this parable, taught his disciples to be prepared to offer personal forgiveness without any limit.' – However, is forgiveness ever easy or without personal cost?

4. 'As his creatures, we have failed to obey even the Lord God's most basic command to live in a way that brings honour to his name; to honour, love and obey him.' – If we are honest, would we find ourselves guilty?

5. 'Having ourselves pleaded for mercy, and been granted great and free forgiveness, we have bound ourselves to show mercy and forgiveness to our fellow believers.' – Do we find ourselves as keen to forgive others as we are keen to be forgiven?

6. 'If we are defrauded or are victims of theft or violence, it is not for us to offer 'cheap' forgiveness. The matter needs to be put in the hands of those who maintain the law, or the offender will be encouraged to take advantage of us and of others and commit further crimes. But it is for us to bear no malice, to seek the welfare of the wrongdoers and to do all that is in our power to encourage those who are guilty to repent before God and live a godly life in future.' – How might these things work out in practice?

7. 'We must learn to forgive them from the heart and not just with our mouth as we secretly plan our revenge!' – How easy is it to do this? If we do not genuinely forgive them, are we are putting into question our own profession of faith?

8. 'True repentance before the Lord God has consequences, it is always costly. It involves an ongoing turning away from wrong doing, and every effort made to put right the wrongs done.' – How true is it that true repentance can be costly?

9. 'As the parable makes plain, having begged for the forgiveness of Almighty God and in mercy been given it, we bind ourselves to be-

ing kind, merciful, patient and forgiving to those around us. In truth, a willingness to forgive 'from the heart' is the hallmark of the true believer.' – Isn't it more natural and easy to 'take offence? 'How are we doing? How well is our church or fellowship doing?

References

'Slaves,' Joseph – Genesis 41:38-44 and Daniel – Daniel 6:1-3
Solomon's magnificent temple cost 3005 talents – 1 Chronicles 29 4-7
As we forgive those who trespass against us – Matthew 6 12-15
Seven times, saying, 'I repent,' you must forgive him – Luke 17:3-4,
Demonstrating 'fruits in keeping with repentance.' – Luke 3:8

The Vineyard Workers

The parable of the vineyard workers follows the record of the encounter with the rich young ruler.

'. . . Jesus said [to the rich young ruler], "You shall not murder, You shall not commit adultery, You shall not steal, You shall not bear false witness, Honour your father and your mother, and, You shall love your neighbour as yourself." The young man said to him, "All these I have kept. What do I still lack?" Jesus said to him, "If you would be perfect, go, sell what you possess and give to the poor, and you will have treasure in heaven; and come, follow me." When the young man heard this he went away sorrowful, for he had great possessions.

And Jesus said to his disciples, "Truly, I say to you, only with difficulty will a rich person enter the kingdom of heaven. Again I tell you, it is easier for a camel to go through the eye of a needle than for a rich person to enter the kingdom of God." When the disciples heard this, they were greatly astonished, saying, "Who then can be saved?" But Jesus looked at them and said, "With man this is impossible, but with God all things are possible." Then Peter said in reply, "See, we have left everything and followed you. What then will we have?" Jesus said to them, "Truly I say to you, in the new world, when the Son of Man will sit on his throne, you who have followed me will also sit on twelve thrones, judging the twelve tribes of Israel. And everyone who has left houses or brothers or sisters or father or mother or children or lands, for my name's sake, will receive a hundredfold and will inherit eternal life. But many who are first will be last, and the last first."'

Matthew 19:18-30 English Standard Version

"For the kingdom of heaven is like a master of a house who went out early in the morning to hire labourers for his vineyard. After agreeing with the labourers for a denarius a day, he sent them into his vineyard. And going out about the third hour he saw others standing idle in the market place, and to them he said, 'You go into the vineyard too, and whatever is right I will give you.' So they went. Going out about the sixth hour and the ninth hour, he did the same. And about the eleventh hour he went out and found others standing. And he said to them, 'Why do you stand here idle all day?' They said to him, 'Because no one has hired us.' He said to them, 'You go into the vineyard too.' And when evening came, the owner of the vineyard said to his foreman, 'Call the labourers and pay them their wages, beginning with the last, up to the first.' And when those hired about the eleventh hour came, each of them received a denarius. Now when those hired first came, they thought they would receive more, but each of them also received a denarius. And on receiving it they grumbled at the master of the house, saying, 'These last worked only one hour, and you have made them equal to us who have borne the burden of the day and the scorching heat.' But he replied to one of them, 'Friend, I am doing you no wrong. Did you not agree with me for a denarius?' Take what belongs to you and go. I choose to give to this last worker as I give to you. Am I not allowed to do what I choose with what belongs to me? Or do you begrudge my generosity?' So the last will be first, and the first last."

Matthew 20:1-16 English Standard Version

The Workers in the Vineyard

Very few of Jesus' parables have caused so much distress and debate as this one!

Read on its own, the parable provokes the reaction, "Why do the first workers not get more? Why should the late-joining workers get the same? It is unfair that those who only worked an hour should be paid as much as those who worked the full twelve hours of the day!"

Richard Trench comments that the parable so distresses our human thinking that, over the centuries, a variety of interpretations have been suggested to make the parable fit what we think it ought to say! It has been suggested that perhaps the late arrivals worked much harder, or maybe the early ones grew slack. It has even been suggested that the denarius, the agreed payment for the day's work, varied in value, with the ones given to the earlier workers being of greater value!

However, our modern Bibles have set us something of a trap. The chapter divisions and the verses help us refer easily to particular teachings or sayings – but they are not part of the original text. On this occasion the chapter division can easily mislead us, causing us to try to understand the parable of the vineyard workers, recorded in chapter 20, without reference to what has been said in the chapter before.

The setting of the parable

In chapter 19 Matthew records that a wealthy young man, who had shaped his life in obedience to the commandments of God, asked what further he should do to inherit eternal life. In his particular situation, Jesus set before him the challenge to tear himself from his great wealth and become a disciple. For the rich young man, that was too painful to contemplate, so he turned away sorrowful.

'And Jesus said to his disciples "Truly, I say to you, only with difficulty will a rich person enter the kingdom of heaven. Again I tell you, it is easier for a camel to go through the eye of a needle than for a rich person to enter the kingdom of God." When the disciples heard this, they were greatly astonished, saying, "Who then can be saved?"' In the disciples' eyes, a wealthy, good-living young man would be an asset to any kingdom, so surely he would have been a valuable member of the kingdom of God.

Peter, as usual speaking for them all, seeing that he and his fellow disciples had done exactly what Jesus had asked of the young man, asks, "See, we have left everything and followed you. What then will we have?"

Jesus' answer assured the disciples that there would be great reward for those who gave up all to follow him – but surprises too, "Truly I say to you, in the new world, when the Son of Man will sit on his throne, you who have followed me will also sit on twelve thrones, judging the twelve tribes of Israel. And everyone who has left houses or brothers or sisters or father or mother or children or lands, for my name's sake, will receive a hundredfold, and will inherit eternal life. But many who are first will be last, and the last first."

Reading chapters 19 and 20 of Matthew's gospel together, it becomes clear that the parable of the vineyard workers is a continuation of the conversation Jesus was having with his disciples, and was specifically addressed to them. If we overlook that setting, the parable on its own can only cause us distress and difficulty.

Some details of the parable
William Barclay explains that in the autumn, once the grapes had ripened, a vineyard owner would hire as many helpers as possible to gather the grapes before the late autumn rains spoiled them.

The market place was the 'job centre' of the ancient world. Men would go there for sunrise, about six in the morning, to be hired for a day's work. The working day lasted until approximately six in the evening. Day workers were dependent for their living on being hired and so some were willing to wait for what little they could earn, even until late in the day.

Having hired workers for an agreed wage at the beginning of the day, but needing to gather all the grapes as soon as possible, the owner went out and hired more workers at about 9am (the third hour) 12noon (the sixth hour) and even at 5pm (the eleventh hour).

Although only the first and last to be paid are mentioned in the parable, it is reasonable to assume that the others too received the same amount.

Scholars debate who the 'foreman' might represent, and why he was only involved in the final payment of the workers rather than involved in their being hired and agreeing their reward. These things do not lie at the heart of the parable and the answers are simply not known.

The conversation with the first workers

'They thought they would receive more.' The first workers had worked for the whole day for an agreed sum of money. However, seeing their employer's generosity to the other workers, they assumed that they would be paid more than that. They wanted not only the sum they had agreed and was rightly theirs, but more than those who worked fewer hours.

The owner's answer was formal and firm, but not necessarily unfriendly. ('Friend' was said to the man at the king's wedding feast who did not have a wedding garment, and to Judas as he came to betray Jesus.) 'Friend, I am doing you no wrong.' The first workers murmured on the basis of what they now felt they should have, but the owner of the vineyard answered on the basis of the amount they had agreed, 'Take what is rightly yours and go . . .'

The immediate challenge of the parable to the disciples

Hidden behind Peter's question, "What then will we have?" (Matt. 19 v. 27) is something that reflects our fallen human nature – our sharp, self-centred sense of what we think we deserve, 'We are not getting what we believe we should have.'

The parable answered both Peter's expectation of honour and reward, and his implied superiority over rich young ruler. (Matt. 19 v. 21-22) As G Campbell Morgan puts it, 'He has turned away, but we have left everything – what will be our reward, what shall we have?'

By way of the parable, William Hendriksen comments, Jesus warned his disciples to beware of applying this kind of worldly thinking to the ways of the kingdom of heaven:

– They were to beware of a worldly 'I'll work, but what will I have for doing so?' attitude.

– They were to acknowledge that the Lord God, who is 'the owner of the kingdom of heaven', has an absolute right to do as he will with his own and that honours and rewards will be given as he chooses.

– They were to beware of a grumbling and self-centered, soul-destroying envy of other workers in God's kingdom whose rewards and honours may be greater than their own.

Jesus had assured the disciples that they would be generously rewarded, they would 'receive a hundredfold'. However, there would be other disciples, perhaps added in later years – as was the apostle Paul – or even added from among the despised Gentiles, who would be even more greatly honoured and rewarded. The last would indeed become first and the first last. Unlike the earliest workers in the vineyard, when they found this to be the case, the disciples were to beware of envy and evil thinking.

The ongoing challenge of the parable

Jesus introduced the parable by saying, 'For the kingdom of heaven is like . . .', and so the parable is a picture of the Lord God as 'owner', and of his dealings 'with his own'.

Are there lessons in this parable for us, and for godly living in our day?'

Firstly, there is a clear warning here to beware of thinking the Lord God ought to do what we think he should do!

Speaking for his Lord, God's prophet Isaiah proclaimed, 'For my thoughts are not your thoughts, neither are your ways my ways,' declares the Lord. 'For as the heavens are higher than the earth, so are my ways higher than your ways and my thoughts than your thoughts.' (Isaiah 55:8-9)

John Calvin comments, ' . . . God is not limited to any person, but calls freely whomsoever He pleases, and bestows on those who are called whatever rewards He thinks fit.'

'Am I not allowed to do what I choose with what belongs to me?'

Peter's question, "See, we have left everything and followed you. What then will we have?" caused our Lord to confront the disciples, and ourselves, with those occasions when our human sense of what is right, comes into conflict with the sovereign will of God to do as he chooses with his own.

Disciples then, and now, are called to acknowledge that the Lord God is our 'Owner', and that the Sovereign Creator God has an absolute right to do as he chooses. This theme of the sovereignty of God runs throughout the Scriptures.

For example: The Lord God chose the people of Israel, although it was the smallest of the nations. Later, he chose David, the youngest son of Jesse, to be the future king of Israel over and above his more mature brothers.

The apostle Paul writes that the Lord God has a right to do as he chooses; he has a right to have mercy on whom he will, just as the potter has the right to do as he will with his clay.

For us, Lord God 'doing what is right with his own' would include our world, our nation and ourselves.

This world is the Lord God's world and he is working out his sovereign purposes for it. The majority of the world's people are either unaware that we live in God's world and are answerable to him for the way we choose to live, or, as in the secular West, choose to ignore him, and so live in rebellion against him. We much prefer to live our lives 'our way,' doing whatever we think is best for us. We much prefer to live our lives 'our way,' doing whatever we think is best for us.

And yet, for each one of us, our existence here and hereafter is in the Lord God's hand: Our life and length of days. All our circumstances – our health, our wealth, our career and our position among our fellow human beings. And finally, our eternal destiny – to be welcomed as a 'good and faithful servant' and so be 'with the Lord,' or in just judgement, to be excluded from his presence. All this is in his hand.

If we are willing to gladly submit to the consistent teaching of Scripture, this understanding of our position in the world is something very wonderful.

However like us, the disciples had much to learn, and much of this fallen world's thinking to 'unlearn'. Peter's question, "What then shall we have?" very much belonged to 'this world's thinking.

The disciples were to become first fruits of God's new creation, his kingdom on earth. They were to be commissioned as the 'heralds of God' carrying the gospel call of repentance before God, submission to his rule and belief in his crucified and risen Son to all nations.

The Lord God's great purpose on earth is to call out from every nation, a people who will gladly live in submission to his rule and governance:

– A people who will live in obedience to his commandments and Fatherly instructions, and the commandments and instructions of his Son, the One who told this parable.

– A people who will live in harmony with him, in harmony with one another and in harmony with this beautiful but spoiled and hurting planet on which he has set us.

– Like the men in the market place, a people ready and looking for opportunities to work for him 'in his vineyard'.

To such people our Lord has promised his guiding hand on our circumstances, here and now, and a place in the kingdom of heaven. They and they alone, 'will inherit eternal life.'

'You go into the vineyard too . . .'
It is human nature to always want more, to be dissatisfied with what we have. But, John the Baptist challenged the soldiers who came to be baptised by him, to show the fruit of true repentance – a humble submission to God's rule and provision – by being 'content with your wages.'

Here is a second lesson for godly living and godly service; it is the precious jewel of godly contentment.

Jesus had promised his disciples that they would 'receive a hundredfold and will inherit eternal life'. The parable was a challenge to them, and to those of us who believe through their testimony, to live content to know that in every circumstance of life the Lord God, who has called us to work in his vineyard will 'give us what is right', not only hereafter, but in his service in this present world too. In the words of Tate and Brady's hymn,

> *Make you His service your delight,*
> *Your wants shall be his care.*

The owner of the vineyard, although he was not to be taken advantage of, was a 'good lord' who clearly looked after the welfare of those he had called to work in his vineyard. Recognising that day workers depend for their living on what little they could earn each day, he was very generous towards the later workers. Yet he also treated those who had first come to an agreement regarding their wages absolutely fairly, he 'did them no wrong'.

Those who accept the call to work for the Lord God can safely trust him, who is 'the best of employers', to be both generous and fair. In their work for him, he can be trusted to direct them to the place of his choosing and to provide all that is necessary to undertake the task he has given them.

Accepting the call he has given to serve him in his 'vineyard', we can live content with the situation in which the Lord has placed us; our family circumstances, our financial status and with the place where we are called to live and work. Here lies the precious jewel of Christian contentment.

Such contentment does not mean that we have no hopes, ambitions or will to strive for justice, far from it. But it does mean that we will seek to contentedly serve the Lord in every situation he puts us; as a youngster, student, parent, Prime Minister or President.

In John Newton's words, we can trust the Lord to, 'supply our wants and direct our steps'. We can trust him lead us as he chooses, and to provide for our needs.

Here is the practical out-working of the Lord's teaching and promise to his true disciples, given in the Sermon on the Mount, 'Therefore do not be anxious, saying, "What shall we eat?' or 'What shall we drink?' or 'What shall we wear?' For the Gentiles seek after all these things, and your heavenly Father knows that you need them all. But seek first the kingdom of God and his righteousness [his wise and right way], and all these things will be added to you.'

As he obeyed the Lord's calling, followed the Lord's directing and travelled on his great missionary journeys, the apostle Paul had learned this great lesson of godly contentment. In grateful thanksgiving to God, Paul could write to the Philippian Christians who, as they were able, sent support to him, '. . . I have learned in whatever situation I am in to be content . . . I have learned the secret of facing plenty and hunger, abundance and need.'

'Whatever is right I will give you'
Here is the third lesson for godly living and service that can be drawn from the parable – the servant's attitude to the Lord God's ultimate reward.

Some of the workers had waited for hours in the market place, hoping to be hired. When later in the day the owner asked them to go and work in the vineyard, they did not focus on the amount they were expecting to receive. These workers were willing to play their part but were not given opportunity until later in the day. But when it was given, they faithfully obeyed and trusted the owner to give them 'what was right'. Like them, we are to make no attempt to bargain, but to rest in the Lord's goodness to give us 'what is right' both in this world and in the world to come.

Towards the end of his life Paul could write to Timothy, 'I have fought the good fight, I have finished the race, I have kept the faith. Henceforth there is laid up for me the crown of righteousness, which the Lord, the righteous judge, will award to me on that Day, and not only to me but also to all who have loved his appearing.'

As the Greek makes plain, the 'crown' Paul had in mind was not the crown of a prince, but that of the successful, winning athlete who had run the race and completed the course. As the apostle Paul laboured for his Lord, bringing the Gospel to the Gentile world, he looked forward to this heavenly honour for his faithful service.

Like the later workers in the parable, as the opportunity allows, we too are called to do what we can, while we can, for the Lord. In John Newton's words, to make use of every opportunity given us 'to promote his cause and encourage his people.'

At the end of our earthly life, what a crowning joy, what an honour it would be to hear something like those words of the Lord Jesus spoken in the parable of the talents, 'Well done, good and faithful servant . . . enter into the joy of your Lord.'

Heavenly Father, give us wisdom to put aside the perceived difficulties we see in this parable, and the humility to learn for ourselves the great lessons you were teaching the disciples.

Questions for reflection or group discussion

1. Like Peter with regard to the rich young ruler, do we sometimes feel that we should be shown greater favour and given greater reward and recognition than someone else?

2. Again like Peter and like the first workers in the vineyard, do we sometimes attempt to come to an agreement with the Lord, 'What will you give me if I do that?' or, 'I'll do this for you if you will give me that.' Or perhaps, 'If you rescue me from this . . ., I'll . . .'

3. How easy is it to consider our own abilities and achievements without a degree of pride? Or to consider the achievements and rewards given to others without a degree of envy?

4. It is hard to put aside all the tricky and contentious issues this parable raises. However, doing so enables us to come face to face with the even more difficult lesson Jesus was teaching the disciples – the owner's right to 'do as he will with his own'. Do we like it when the Lord God's right to 'do as he will' restricts or frustrates our own plans, schemes, and ambitions?

5. How can we learn to submit to the rule of the Lord God in our lives and, even more difficult for wayward and rebellious human beings, learn to be content under it?

6. How hard is it simply to trust the Lord to give us what is right?

7. As the final workers may have felt, do we sometimes find ourselves all but overwhelmed with the Lord God's patience, kindness and generosity towards us? Might that be a foretaste of heaven?

References

The potter and his clay – Romans 9:20-21

The Lord God chose Israel . . . the smallest – Deut 7:6 and 14:2.

He chose David, the youngest son of Jesse – 1 Sam 16:6-12

Who loved us and gave himself for us – Galatians 2:20

The disciples commissioned – Matthew 28:19-20, Luke 24:46-52, Acts 1:8-11

The Lord God, in whose hand is our breath – Daniel 5:23

John the Baptist, be content with your wages – Luke 3:14
Serve the Lord with gladness – Psalm 100:2
Therefore do not be anxious – Matthew 6:31-33
I have learned . . . to be content – Philippians 4:11-12
I have fought the good fight – 2 Timothy 4:7-8
Well done good and faithful servant – Matthew 25:21
Make you his service your delight – lines from *Through all the changing scenes of life* 1696 version, Nahum Tate 1652-1715 and Nicholas Brady 1659-1726

Words of Jesus associated with this parable

'The last shall be first . . .'
This saying is recorded both immediately before the parable and is repeated immediately after it. Many commentators have been greatly troubled by the saying and have suggested reasons to ignore it or attempted to 'soften' it.

However, it cannot just be applied to the order in which they were paid as Origen suggested. Nor can it be done away with by suggesting that its repeated use is somehow misplaced in the gospel and so can be safely passed over as not being connected with the parable.

The saying is far more challenging. It is a solemn warning concerning the attitude displayed by Peter, 'Having given up everything, we are more worthy than the rich young ruler. What will we get?' and by the first workers who murmured thinking, 'having worked all through the day, we are worthy of more money than these others.' As the apostle Paul writes, we will still be given eternal life by the grace of the Lord God, but all our efforts in apparently godly work that are founded on self-centred motives will be burned up as mere 'wood, hay and stubble. (1 Corinthians 3:12-15)

Towards the end of the Sermon on the Mount, Jesus solemnly warned that, if our motives are fundamentally self-centred, despite preaching, teaching and performing wonderful things in his name, we may finally hear the dreadful words, 'I never knew you; depart from me . . .' (Matthew 7:23)

This saying, of Jesus 'The first shall be last . . .' is also recorded in Luke 13:22-30, where the words are applied to the unbelieving Jewish leaders, '. . . there will be weeping and gnashing of teeth, when you see Abraham and Isaac and Jacob and all the prophets in the kingdom of God but you yourselves cast out. And people will come from east and west, and from north and south, and recline at table in the kingdom of God. And behold, some are last who will be first, and some are first who will be last.'

For the future, the saying would also be a word to the Jewish believers who were to find it so hard to accept Gentile believers as true brothers and sisters, fellow citizens of the kingdom of heaven, some of whom would ultimately outshine even the most illustrious of Jewish believers.

'For many are called but few are chosen'
These words are found in some ancient manuscripts and are recorded in the Authorised, King James Version but are usually omitted in modern Bible editions. Although some texts omit them, the words fit perfectly as the conclusion of the parable when we see that they refer back to the rich young ruler and Jesus' warning to the disciples of the difficulty of leaving the ties of this world to single-mindedly follow him. The saying spells out the difficulty of obeying and following him when the cost is high. Yet it is plain that his chosen ones will count all else as worth nothing, 'dung,' in comparison with 'the surpassing worth of knowing Christ Jesus my Lord . . .' as the apostle Paul and his fellow apostles gladly did when they had been enlightened and empowered by the Holy Spirit of God. (Philippians 3:8)

These words of Jesus, 'For many are called, but few are chosen' are also recorded in Matthew 22:14 in the parable of the marriage of the king's son, where the meaning is clear. It is applied to the true guests in contrast to the man who joined the banquet in some unauthorised way and so did not have the wedding garment provided for invited guests.

Footnotes – light from other Scriptures

1. Although it goes against our perception of 'what is deserved', the gifts of God are always of grace and never because of our merit. To be 'with the Lord' was given to the apostle Paul, who by his own confession 'laboured more' than any of the other apostles, as well as to the thief on the cross who had little or no opportunity to labour at all. (1 Corinthians 15:10 and Luke 23:43)

2. Disciples, then and now are challenged not to be like the dissatisfied workers who were first to begin work in the vineyard. We are called to be content and not to compare – as Peter did as he compared himself and his fellow disciples with the rich young ruler, and as Peter did again when he met he risen Lord by the lake, when he asked Jesus about John's future, 'What will happen to him?'(John 21:21-22) We see this same envy in the disciples in their displeasure at discovering that James and John had attempted to secure the 'top positions' in their Lord's future kingdom. (Mark 10:35-45)

3. We are called to learn to be content in all our circumstances, as the apostle Paul had done. Another way of putting it would be to 'take his yoke on ourselves and learn of him', willingly, contentedly, submitting to his rule and guiding, his leading and the burden his gives us to bear, knowing that he will give us what is best for us. (Matthew 11:28-30)

Further brief notes

1. In the parable, the first workers made an agreement. Later workers did not have an agreement, they simply trusted the owner's word to 'give them whatever is right'. To the last group of workers, the owner does not promise anything, he simply invites them to go and work in his vineyard, so their trust in the owner was complete. Those who

showed the greatest trust had the greatest cause for thanksgiving and rejoicing – the last were indeed first and the first last.

2. The parable was addressed to the future apostles who were the first to be called to work in Christ's vineyard. They worked in it tirelessly and at great personal cost. Yet many of them lived to see that 'late arrival,' the apostle Paul, rise to become the great apostle to the Gentiles.

3. Some of the early church leaders saw the parable reflecting the different ages through which the people of God have passed, from the call of Abraham, to the times of the prophets, to the call of the apostles and to the final hour, days of grace in which we live.

4. Why did the owner decide to pay last first? It would enable those who had started earlier to be aware of the generosity of the owner to the later workers, and illustrate the first being made last.

5. Commenting on the words 'they murmured' Richard Trench challenged his readers to watch out for all inclinations to pride ourselves on our own doings, as though they gave us a claim on God.

The Two Sons

And when he entered the temple, the chief priests and the elders of the people came up to him as he was teaching, and said, "By what authority are you doing these things, and who gave you this authority?" Jesus answered them, "I also will ask you one question, and if you tell me the answer, I also will tell you by what authority I do these things. The baptism of John, from where did it come? From heaven or from man?" And they discussed it among themselves, saying, "If we say, 'From heaven,' he will say to us, 'Why then did you not believe him?' But if we say, 'From man,' we are afraid of the crowd, for they all hold that John was a prophet." So they answered Jesus, "We do not know." And he said to them, "Neither will I tell you by what authority I do these things."

"What do you think? A man had two sons. And he went to the first and said, 'Son, go and work in the vineyard today.' And he answered, 'I will not,' but afterwards he changed his mind and went. And he went to the other son and said the same. And he answered, 'I will go, sir,' but did not go. Which of the two did the will of his father?" They said, "The first." Jesus said to them, "Truly, I say to you, the tax collectors and the prostitutes go into the kingdom of God before you. For John came to you in the way of righteousness, and you did not believe him, but the tax collectors and prostitutes believed him. And even when you saw it, you did not afterward change your minds and believe him."

Matthew 21:23-32 English Standard Version

The Parable of the Two Sons

Introduction to these parables

The parable of the two sons is the first of three parables told by Jesus in the temple in Jerusalem during the final days of his ministry. The parables were not addressed to the disciples, or to the people he was teaching in the temple at the time. They were part of Jesus' reply to the Pharisees and elders of the people, as a delegation of them came and interrupted his teaching. They came to challenge him concerning his authority to do all the things he was doing, and so these parables are addressed specifically to them.

Already in their thinking was their determination to be rid of him; to kill him. This series of parables was Jesus' final plea to them to turn from their mistaken rejection of him as the Messiah, and so avoid the judgment of God – the forfeiture of their privileged position, the end of their sacrificial ministry, the destruction of the temple, and the loss of their own lives.

(In A.D 70, the Romans brought about this judgement as they captured Jerusalem and reduced it to a pile of rubble.)

The parables of the two sons, the vineyard tenants and the wedding feast of the king's son, contain increasingly strong warnings to them. By these parables, Jesus was as it were holding up a mirror to enable the religious leaders to see for themselves what they were doing and the consequences of it.

An inquiry with the full weight of the law

'And when he entered the temple, the chief priests and the elders of the people came up to him as he was teaching, and said, "By what authority are you doing these things, and who gave you this authority?"'

Here was the man who had dared to clear the temple of the lucrative market – a market which was held in the temple court set aside as a place where non-Jewish people could come and pray. Here he was again in one of the temple courts publicly teaching the people, and by his whole manner stirring the people to question the authority of the religious leaders. Their authority would be undermined if this continued, so they challenged him by demanding to know by what authority he did these things, and who gave it to him. They knew that he had not sought their permission, nor had they given him authority to clear the temple or to teach within its courts. By their questions, their intention was to bring an immediate end his 'irregular' ministry and challenge to their authority.

Jesus answered them, "I also will ask you one question, and if you tell me the answer, I also will tell you by what authority I do these things. The baptism of John, from where did it come? From heaven or from man?"

Jesus did not directly answer their questions, but pointed them to the ministry of John the Baptist. He was not 'evading the question' but was fully aware that the mind of the temple authorities was closed to the truth. It would have been both pointless and inappropriate to tell them plainly of his divine origin and appointment. But, if they were in any way open to the truth, he did give them the answer to their aggressive legal questioning by pointing them to John.

John was the son of the priest Zechariah, who with his wife Elizabeth had been unable to have children. As a correction for doubting the word of the Lord delivered by an angel of God, and as a sign that the Lord God would fulfil his word and give them a son, John's father Zechariah was struck dumb. Later, when asked to name his new-born son, Zechariah resisted the pressure to call him by a familiar family name and obeyed the word of the Lord, given by the angel, naming him 'John'. Immediately his tongue was set free and he declared by a prophecy that his son John, known to us as John the Baptist, would be the herald of the Lord God. He would call the people of Israel to repent and to prepare for the arrival of Israel's Redeemer; the promised Messiah. (Luke 1:57-79)

Zechariah had been struck dumb while ministering as a priest in the temple, and so these things would have been known to the temple authorities.

As a grown man, John fulfilled the role of herald as he bore witness to Jesus as the 'the One who was to come', the Messiah, the 'Son of God'. The ordinary people recognised John to be a prophet of God, and great crowds of them flocked to hear him. Many of them turned from ungodly ways and were baptised. However, the temple authorities, together with the majority of the scribes and Pharisees, although they were aware of these things, had no eyes to see or ears to hear what the Lord God was doing.

Why were the chief priests and Pharisees so unable to see?
The chief priests and elders in Jerusalem were, as they saw it, 'at the centre of national religious and political life'. Although occupying the position of the most senior shepherds of God's people, the chief priests and Pharisees in Jerusalem were in practice power-holding political leaders under the Romans.

In such a state of mind and heart, they found themselves bound. They could not afford to acknowledge what God was doing by his servant John in preparing the people of Israel for the arrival of God's anointed One, the Messiah. And they could not afford to recognise that the Lord Jesus, to whom John bore witness, was the promised Messiah.

Secretly they were aware of it, as Nicodemus, a member of this same ruling party, acknowledged when he came to Jesus by night, "Rabbi, we know that you are a teacher come from God, for no one can do these signs that you do unless God is with him." However, publicly they denied it. The chief priests and Pharisees were living in wilful denial, and determinedly would not 'change their minds'.

This is the reason why our Lord did not give them a direct answer to their question – 'And they discussed it among themselves, saying "If we say, 'From heaven,' he will say to us, 'Why then did you not believe him?' But if we say, 'From man,' we are afraid of the crowd, for they all hold that John was a prophet." So they answered Jesus, "We do not know." And he said to them, "Neither will I tell you by what authority I do these things."'

The temple authorities condemned themselves. They could not afford to answer that John's authority was from God, for that would call for their recognition of him as a prophet of God, and for their own need to heed his call to humble themselves, repent and prepare for the arrival of the Messiah. Nor could they afford to answer that John did not have such God-given authority, so they gave a wilfully blind and less-than-honest answer, "We do not know."

This is the setting of the parable of the two sons which immediately follows this legal inquiry and interchange with the temple authorities and is a part of the same conversation.

The parable of the two sons

"What do you think? A man had two sons. And he went to the first and said, 'Son go and work in the vineyard today.' And he answered, 'I will not,' but afterwards he changed his mind and went. And he went to the other son and said the same. And he answered, 'I will go, sir,' but did not go. Which of the two did the will of his father?" They said, "The first." Jesus said to them, "Truly, I say to you, the tax collectors and the prostitutes go into the kingdom of God before you. For John came to you in the way of righteousness, and you did not believe him, but the tax collectors and prostitutes believed him.

Like the tax-gatherers who made an ungodly choice in their career, the first son made a disobedient choice and refused to obey his father. However, on reflection this son realised his mistake and went to work in the vineyard.

The second son was different, he answered, 'I will go, sir,' or 'I, sir,' as it is in the Greek. It is an expression which means 'certainly, sir,' 'you may depend on me, sir,' 'I'm ready and willing to go.' Possibly, Jesus used this expression to draw out the contrast between the two sons. From his words in response to his father's request, this second son appeared to be the 'ideal son' – respectful, obedient and happy to fulfil his father's wishes. However, in practice, he was very far from it. Despite his willing words, he ignored his father and did not go to work in the in the vineyard.

The examiners examined
By asking them, 'Which son did his father's will?' Jesus invited the chief priests and Pharisees to be the judges in their own case. They came to interrogate Jesus, but were themselves given a soul-searching challenge. The Pharisees' publicly declared aim was to obey the Lord God in every detail of each commandment – and yet, like the second son, in practice they fell very far short of that. They 'honoured him with their lips, but their hearts were far from him'.

Jesus said to them, ". . . John came to you in the way of righteousness, and you did not believe him, but the tax collectors and prostitutes believed him. And even when you saw it, you did not afterward change your minds and believe him.'

Under the God-anointed preaching of John, even hardened tax-gatherers and prostitutes discovered themselves to have fallen far short before God. Acknowledging and confessing it, they were baptised by John with a baptism of repentance, resolving to turn from their ungodly ways. The visible result of John's ministry was a great number of people whose lives had been totally turned around, as they genuinely turned from ungodliness of living to an obedient and God-pleasing way of life – 'the way of righteousness'.

With such a message so effectively and publicly proclaimed, the religious leaders should surely have welcomed John, agreed with him and acknowledged that he was a prophet raised up of God for such a time – but they did not.

The leaders were aware of these things and yet remained wilfully stubborn in their refusal to recognise John's God-given calling and authority.

In the same way the hearts of the religious leaders remained wilfully hardened against the One to whom John bore witness, and whose herald he was. They were aware of the witness John bore to Jesus, as well as the witness of Simeon and Anna as they spoke of the young Jesus in the temple. They heard, or heard reports of Jesus' teaching, and were aware of his mighty miracles which were clear signs of his being the long promised Messiah. But they remained unmoved. He was a threat to their hollow profession of perfect obedience to the Lord God. He was also a threat to the respect in which the ordinary people held them, and so a threat to their high position in society.

By referring them to John the Baptist, and by this parable of the two sons, Jesus fully answered the question concerning his authority. If the senior religious leaders in the temple had acknowledged John to be a prophet of God, they would also have recognised the One to whom he bore witness, namely Jesus. They chose to recognise neither of them.

Like the second son, their profession of godly obedience was an empty one, full of fine words when their hearts were very far from God and a godly submission to him and his ways.

Lessons for ourselves in our day
Although the parable was addressed to the temple authorities so many years ago, this incident in the temple, and our Lord's short parable of the two sons, offer us a great encouragement and a great challenge.

What an encouragement is the ministry of John the Baptist for those of us who have made very serious errors in life, and perhaps tumbled into very ungodly ways. There is no depth to which we may have fallen but the rescuing mercy and love of God is not deeper. The Lord God is well able to rescue, forgive and give a fresh new start to those who humble themselves and come in repentance to him for mercy and forgiveness.

It was for the encouragement of just such people that the apostle Paul, writing to the Christians in the port city of Corinth, where immorality and ungodly ways were widespread, was moved to write, '. . . and such were some of you. But you have been washed, you have been sanctified, you have been justified in the name of the Lord Jesus Christ and by the Spirit of our God.'

As an example of the depth to which the Lord God's mercy reaches, Paul wrote of himself, 'The saying is trustworthy and deserving full acceptance, that Christ Jesus came into the world to save sinners, of whom I am the foremost.'

Paul viewed himself as the foremost, the worst, the chief of sinners. As a proud Pharisee he had attempted, by arrest and imprisonment, to violently stamp out the faith he later proclaimed; the gospel message of repentance, forgiveness and 'faith in the Son of God who loved me and gave himself for me.' From his own example, Paul displayed that none have fallen too low to be rescued and forgiven.

Jesus' encounter with the religious leaders in the temple is an encouragement, too, for those who reach out with the gospel, seeking to help others to come to faith. The Lord God is well able to take the feeble words of his people and use them for his glory. Our Lord speaks of 'the tax collectors and the prostitutes going into the kingdom of God' – believing and responding to John's message in repentance and faith.

The religious leaders had long 'written off' tax-gatherers and sinners as being hopeless, 'soiled beyond redemption'. They despised such people, and would have nothing to do with them, in case they themselves became 'ritually unclean'.

However, here were people, made in the image of God, who had fallen into ungodly lifestyles, and the Lord alone knows the secret cries of our human hearts. Some of them may have had deep longings to escape. It was by the faithful preaching of John, that the Holy Spirit brought rescue – repentance, forgiveness and a new God-pleasing life, to the most hardened and unlikely of people.

Words that are a challenge
The great challenge of the parable of the two sons for those of us who profess and call ourselves Christian believers, is to look to ourselves and see if our faith is real, deep and consistent throughout our whole life, or merely – as it was for so many of the religious leaders of Jesus' time, an outward display – a veneer, only surface deep.

Like the second son, we can offer pleasing words when the occasion arises, and yet not follow them through in practical, everyday living. When we are not consciously in the presence of the Lord or in the presence of godly people, we may be far from willingly obedient to godly ways. We can live our lives in separate compartments, 'the godly, religious part' but, at home or at work, 'the ordinary, everyday part'.

We, too, just as Jesus said of the scribes and Pharisees, can honour the Lord God with our lips, but have hearts that are far from God and godly ways.

As Harold Lindsell points out, practical obedience to the word of God in the way we live our lives is the great test of faith in every generation.

For those of us called to be leaders of God's people, the challenge of the incident in the temple is even sharper. Over the years, we can become so familiar with godly words and phrases that they just flow from us. Yet behind the public gaze our words may not be matched by godliness in our everyday living – perhaps as we handle financial matters, or manoeuver outcomes to our advantage.

That was exactly the problem with many of the religious leaders of the people of Israel in Jesus' time. They were held in high esteem, yet beneath the religious exterior, they were worldly-minded and greedy for gain. As Jesus put it so strongly, they were 'full of greed and self-indulgence, hypocrisy and lawlessness'. They kept themselves, according to their own traditions, 'ritually pure', and were very concerned to preserve their own privileged position in society. But with minds set on worldly matters and position, they failed to walk closely with the Lord they claimed to serve.

True righteousness is characterised by a humble submission to the word of God as we conform our lives, our attitudes and our dealings with others to its teaching. It displays itself in our lives by openness to reason, patience, kindness and forgiveness of those around us, and in trust, obedience and a dependence on the leading, guiding and overruling of all our circumstances by the Holy Spirit of God.

King David in the fifth psalm, encourages us to pray, 'Lead me, O Lord, in your righteousness because of my enemies; make your way straight before me.' Or put more simply, 'Lead me, O Lord, in your right way, because of my enemies (my pride, stubbornness and hardness of heart from within, and the pressures of the world and the evil one from without) make your way clear and plain before me.'

In conclusion

The parable was addressed to the temple leaders as they sought to end the teaching, and in their eyes 'threatening', ministry of Jesus. But the incident, and the parable our Lord told in response to their questioning, offer to us both great encouragement and a great challenge. An encouragement to humbly repent and seek his face and his forgiveness for all that is past. And a challenge to look to him to open our eyes to see what he is doing in our day and to walk before him in humility, love, obedience and dependence, no matter how exalted our position may be among the men and women of this world.

Heavenly Father, this is an incident and brief parable that is easily passed over as being of no relevance to us in our day. By your grace, enable us to humble ourselves and seek forgiveness for all that is past, and, no matter how highly we may be honoured in society, incline our hearts to walk before you in dependence on your provision and leading, and in love and obedience to you.

Questions for personal reflection or discussion

1. Why would it have been inappropriate for Jesus to give the chief priests and Pharisees a plain and direct answer to their questions?

2. Why is John the Baptist's ministry such an encouragement for those of us who have made very serious errors in life, and perhaps tumbled into very bad ways?

3. Have you known for yourself or know of other people whose lives had been totally turned around under the hand of God?

4. Is it worth pausing and looking closely at each of the three parts of the apostle Paul's gospel message; repentance, forgiveness and faith in the Son of God who loved us and gave himself for us?

5. The Lord God is well able to take the feeble words of his people and use them for his glory. Have we known anything of it ourselves, or seen it happen among our friends?

6. Can we live our lives in separate compartments, 'the godly, religious part' and 'the ordinary, everyday part'? How can we help one another to make the whole of our lives more godly?

7. 'Will we merely say, or will we actually obey?' Practical obedience to the word of God in the way we live our lives is the great test of faith. What can we personally be doing to help us daily to grow in obedience?

8. 'Lead me, O Lord, in your righteousness because of my enemies; (my pride, stubbornness and hardness of heart from within, and the pressures of the world and the evil one from without) make your way clear and plain before me.' Can such a prayer help and encourage us in our daily living?

Footnotes

'The way of righteousness' is a Hebrew expression meaning to be right with the Lord God and living in his right way in his world. It is living in obedience to the Lord God and is also described as 'the way of God' in Matthew 22:16.

J C Ryle comments that he whole incident also serves as a warning. 'By what authority?' is the question often used to challenge and silence true servants of God raised up for 'irregular' ministries. It was the charge used against the Puritans, the Reformers and the early Methodists.

References

Jesus clearing the temple – Matthew 21:12-13

Elizabeth and Zechariah – Luke 1:5-23

John the Baptist; the herald of the Lord God – Luke 1:57-79

The 'the One who was to come,' 'Son of God,' the Messiah – Matthew 3:11-17

Nicodemus, "Rabbi, we know that you are a teacher come from God, for no one can do these signs that you do unless God is with him." – John 3:1-2

Simeon and Anna – Luke 2:25-38

'. . . and such were some of you. But you have been washed, you have been sanctified, you have been justified in the name of the Lord Jesus Christ and by the Spirit of our God.' – 1 Corinthians 6:11

'The saying is trustworthy and deserving full acceptance, that Christ Jesus came into the world to save sinners, of whom I am the foremost.' – 1 Timothy 1:15

'. . . faith in the Son of God who loved us and gave himself for us.' – Galatians 2:20

We, too, can honour the Lord God with our lips but have hearts that are far from God and godly ways – Matthew 15:8 (Isaiah 29:13)

Outwardly they appeared righteous to others, but within were full of greed and self-indulgence, hypocrisy and lawlessness – Matthew 23:25-28

'Lead me, O Lord, in your righteousness' – Psalm 5:8.

The Wedding Feast

When the chief priests and the Pharisees heard his parables, they perceived that he was speaking about them. And although they were seeking to arrest him, they feared the crowds, because they held him to be a prophet.

And again Jesus spoke to them in parables, saying "The kingdom of heaven may be compared to a king who gave a wedding feast for his son, and sent his servants to call those who were invited to the wedding feast, but they would not come. Again he sent other servants, saying, 'Tell those who are invited, See, I have prepared my dinner, my oxen and my fat calves have been slaughtered, and everything is ready. Come to the wedding feast.' But they paid no attention and went off, one to his farm, another to his business, while the rest seized his servants, treated them shamefully, and killed them. The king was angry, and sent his troops and destroyed those murderers and burned their city. Then he said to his servants, 'The wedding feast is ready, but those invited were not worthy. Go therefore to the main roads and invite to the wedding feast as many as you find.' And those servants went out into the roads and gathered all whom they found, both bad and good. So the wedding hall was filled with guests.

But when the king came in to look at the guests, he saw there a man who had no wedding garment. And he said to him, 'Friend, how did you get in here without a wedding garment?' And he was speechless. Then the king said to the attendants, 'Bind him hand and foot and cast him into the outer darkness. In that place there will be weeping and gnashing of teeth.' For many are called, but few are chosen."

Then the Pharisees went and plotted how to entangle him in his talk.

Matthew 21:45 - 22:15, English Standard Version

The Wedding Feast

Introduction

This is the third of the series of parables Jesus gave to the Pharisees, chief priests and elders in the temple in Jerusalem in the last days of his ministry. The parables were increasingly strong in their warnings of what would result from the present thinking of Israel's wilfully blind religious leaders.

Matthew records. 'And when he entered the temple the chief priests and elders of the people came up to him as he was teaching, and said, "By what authority are you doing these things, and who gave you this authority?" (Matthew 21:23) After asking them who gave John the Baptist his authority, Jesus gave these parables. They were given, not to condemn the chief priests and Pharisees, but to enable them to see the seriousness of their intended plan to put him to death, and its consequences for Jerusalem and for themselves – and to call them to turn from it.

The first, the parable of the two sons, began with the question, "What do you think?" It invited them to be the judges of their own case. The second, the parable of the vineyard tenants, began, "Hear another parable." This clearly showed them who he was, what they were planning, and the dire consequences of it. The third and final parable is this parable of the wedding feast.

The two parables of guests invited to a banquet

The parable of the king's marriage feast for his son is very similar to the parable of the great banquet found in Luke's gospel. And it is worthy of note that on each occasion the parable was given as a warning to Israel's religious leaders.

The parable of the great banquet recorded by Luke took place over a meal, during a conversation in a Pharisee's house. It was given much earlier in Jesus' ministry. In that parable the guests excuse themselves and others are gathered from the 'highways and hedges' to take their place.

The parable of the wedding feast for the king's son was given in the temple in Jerusalem during the final days of our Lord's ministry. It was addressed to Israel's most senior religious leaders, and Jesus' description of the loss incurred by the guests who rejected the king's invitation and dishonoured him is far more serious.

The parable of the wedding feast

The parable is in three parts:

The invitations were delivered to the king's honoured guests and they responded at first with apathy and then, on the second invitation, with contempt.

Other, seemingly far less worthy, guests were gathered.

A man was present at the feast who was not wearing the appropriate wedding garment.

The invitations delivered by the king's servants

The king sent out his servants, first to deliver an invitation in good time so that the guests would know they were invited and could prepare themselves and make their way to the feast. However, despite the honour, these guests, as the Greek says, 'did not wish' to go. He then sent out a second invitation, when all was prepared, to urge them to come to the feast. This was the normal way of invitation in days when there were no clocks or diaries.

The invited guests' reception of the second invitation displayed their utter contempt for the king. Ignoring the invitation, 'not caring' as the Greek puts it, one went to his field, and another to his trade. Even worse, the abuse and the killing of some of the servants was a deliberate and dreadful provocation. When an ambassador is insulted, humiliated or worse, the affront is intended, not for him personally, but for the one who sent him. The gospel records that king was well aware of this, and responded by sending his armies to destroy them and their cities.

The result was not just loss of the invited guests' privileged opportunity to dine, but the destruction of their cities and of themselves. By the utter contempt they had shown, they had brought on themselves the full force of a king's wrath.

It is not impossible that by the time Matthew's gospel was written, the Romans had done just this to the rebellious and provocative Jewish people of Jerusalem.

By way of the parable, Jesus was showing the chief priests and Pharisees that he was no upstart claimant to be the Messiah, but the One long promised by the Old Testament prophets, and publicly witnessed to in their own day by the last of the prophets, John the Baptist. John's message was the call to be ready for Israel's crowning glory – the presence of their true Lord and King among them. However, just like the guests invited to the wedding feast of the king's son, Israel's religious leaders refused to recognise John's God-given authority, or to heed his message.

Because of their rejection of both John's witness to the Messiah, and of Israel's Messiah himself, Jesus could see what lay ahead. This is why, just before he left the temple, Jesus said of Jerusalem and its religious leaders, "O Jerusalem, Jerusalem, the city that kills the prophets and stones those who are sent to it! How often would I have gathered your children together as a hen gathers her brood under her wings, and you would not! See, your house is left to you desolate. For I tell you, you will not see me until you say, 'Blessed is he who comes in the name of the Lord.'"

Not only were the Lord God's prophets treated shamefully, but so was Israel's glory, the Son of God himself.

The gathering of others to take the places of the invited guests
The picture of the Lord God's final heavenly banquet was to the forefront in the thinking of Jewish religious leaders in Jesus' time. They spoke of it often and greatly prized their own assumed presence at it, alongside the great ones of Israel's history, Abraham, Isaac, and Jacob.

Alluding to this great heavenly banquet, one of the guests at table in the house of the ruler of the Pharisees said, "Blessed is everyone who will eat bread in the kingdom of God!" Jesus responded to the guest and his fellow religious leaders by challenging the unspoken assumption that they would be there. By way of the parable of the great banquet, he gave them a solemn warning that they might well not be present.

On that occasion, as in this parable of the king's wedding feast, by the picture of others taking the place of the invited guests, our Lord challenged this widely held assumption that they, as Israel's esteemed religious leaders, would 'of course' be there. Even more discomforting, was the suggestion that the people they most despised would be the ones chosen and gathered to take their places.

The honoured guests contemptuously refused to attend, so the king said to his servants, 'The wedding feast is ready, but those invited were not worthy. Go therefore to the main roads and invite to the wedding feast as many as you find.' And those servants went out into the roads and gathered all whom they found, both bad and good. So the wedding hall was filled with guests.'

The servants were sent out to the street corners and crossroads, 'the parting of the ways' as the Greek puts it, where many people would pass, and they gathered them in. They gathered 'both bad and good'; those of whom the religious leaders would approve, and those of whom they most definitely would not. They gathered in 'the righteous', and they also gathered tax collectors and sinners, despised Gentiles and perhaps even some of the soldiers of their Roman conquerors. The banquet hall was filled – but not with themselves and people 'of their own class and standing' as the religious leaders imagined.

The man at the banquet without a festive garment
But when the king came in to look at the guests, he saw there a man who had no wedding garment. And he said to him, 'Friend, how did

you get in here without a wedding garment?' And he was speechless. Then the king said to the attendants, 'Bind him hand and foot and cast him into the outer darkness. In that place there will be weeping and gnashing of teeth.' For many are called, but few are chosen.

The incident of the man without a wedding garment is another of the features that distinguishes this parable from that of the great banquet. The robe for the wedding feast was almost certainly freely provided by the king for his invited guests. The garments were either specially made for the occasion, or provided from his treasury store of 'festal garments'. For this reason, being clothed with it before taking a place at the banquet was a mark of respect for the king. So the presence at the banquet of a man 'not having been dressed in a wedding robe' as the Greek puts it, would indicate one of three things: That the man was an intruder. That he was an invited guest who had somehow entered the banqueting hall without passing through the guests' dressing room. That he was an invited guest who was being deliberately insulting and provocative by refusing to wear the wedding garment.

The King gave the man without a wedding garment an opportunity to explain his situation, but he had nothing to say, the Greek is literally he was 'gagged'. His fallen face and silence were an expression of his shame and discomfort.

The Greek words make a distinction between the servants who invited the guests and the servants the king now calls to remove this unwelcome guest. They are described as 'binders' as they were the king's security officers. Bound hand and foot the intruder is made incapable of any attempt to escape the fate which awaits him – exclusion from the presence of the king and from the feast.

The feast would be brightly lit and magnificent, but on the orders of the king, the contemptuous guest was bound and thrown out – cast out either into the darkness of the street at night, or into some dark prison cell.

Although we can easily over-spiritualise it, the man was thrown into the darkness – to endlessly 'feast' himself on the bitter tears of anger towards himself for his own great misjudgement, and on the endless tears of regret for his act of contempt in failing to honour the king.

How did this part of the parable speak to the chief priests and Pharisees in Jerusalem?
The chief priests and Pharisees would neither recognise John the Baptist as a prophet of God, nor the One of whom John was herald, Israel's true King and Messiah. As a result they would find themselves excluded from the kingdom of God and the great heavenly feast. The consequences of their wilful failure to honour the Lord God and his anointed Son would be terrible.

Just like the man who was unwilling to honour the king by wearing the wedding robe at the marriage feast of his son, the leading Pharisees in Jerusalem proudly assumed that, as Israel's eminent religious leaders, they were worthy of a place in the heavenly banquet just as they were. However, our Lord was warning them that, proud, wilful and unrepentant as they actually were, they would find themselves cast out. There would indeed be weeping and gnashing of teeth – an endless, agonised cry of, 'If only we had listened. If only we had realised. If only we had . . .'

Other occasions when Jesus had given this warning
As he healed the Roman centurion's servant, he said to those who followed him, "Truly, I tell you, with no one in Israel have I found such faith. I tell you, many will come from east and west and recline at table with Abraham, Isaac, and Jacob in the kingdom of heaven, while the sons of the kingdom will be thrown into outer darkness. In that place there will be weeping and gnashing of teeth."

Concluding the parable of the narrow door, Jesus warned that the master of the house will say, 'I tell you, I do not know where you come from. Depart from me, all you workers of evil!' In that place there will be weeping and gnashing of teeth, when you see Abraham and Isaac and Jacob and all the prophets in the kingdom of God but you yourselves cast out. And people will come from east and west, and from north and south, and recline at table in the kingdom of God, and behold, some are last who will be first, and some are first who will be last.

To Israel's eminent religious leaders, the thought of being excluded from the great and final heavenly banquet was unthinkable. And yet it would be fulfilled because, as Jesus said as he wept over Jerusalem, they 'did not recognise the day of their visitation'.

The parable of the wedding feast is at least the third, and certainly the final recorded time that the Lord Jesus warned Israel's religious leaders that they were in danger of being excluded from the heavenly banquet.

However, they did not wish to know; they had no ears to hear.

Lessons from the parable for ourselves in our day

The treatment of the king's messengers

The servants were treated civilly on the first invitation, as were the disciples during our Lord's lifetime. In general, the people of Israel and their religious leaders received the invitation but simply ignored it, as they did the Lord Jesus' own invitation. Their refusal caused him to say to them, "You search the Scriptures because you think that in them you have eternal life; and it is they that bear witness about me, yet you refuse to come to me that you may have life."

Countless people do this in our own day with the invitation of the gospel of God. It is not that we actively hate it or mistreat the messengers. The majority of us simply have deaf ears and unseeing eyes. Like the invited guests of the parable, we 'do not wish' to hear, we are 'not interested', or perhaps we dismiss it because we regard ourselves as 'not religious'.

At the second invitation to notify the invited guests that all was now ready and to urge the guests to come, some of the servants who brought the message were ignored; the guests preferring the overseeing of the farm or their everyday business pursuits. By other guests, the servants were dreadfully mistreated.

As the Scriptures make plain, not only were the Lord God's prophets consistently shamefully treated, but so was the Son of God himself. After the resurrection his chosen messengers, the apostles, also suffered shameful mistreatment, imprisonment, beatings, stoning and death.

As it was in the days of our Lord and his apostles, in our own day it is often religious leaders who attempt to silence those who faithfully teach and proclaim the truth of God's Holy Word.

Richard Trench writes, 'Men's worldliness resists the truth; but there are deeper evils in their hearts, which it will often not fail to arouse. It wounds their pride, it affronts their self-righteousness; and where they dare, they will visit on those that bring it the hate which they bear to itself.'

The gathering in of both bad and good
Philip went down to the despised people of Samaria and preached the gospel to a people who were of very mixed race and faith. Although Peter initially regarded Gentile people as 'unclean' and 'unrighteous,' yet was called of God to preach the gospel to the Roman, Cornelius, and those in his house. To the fury of the self-righteous Jewish religious leaders, Paul proclaimed the gospel to the men of Thessalonica, Berea and to the Gentiles in many other cities.

'Both bad and good'; of the good, Cornelius was already a noble seeker after truth. Of the bad, after a list including drunkards, cheats and thieves, Paul writes of the believers in Corinth, 'And such were some of you. But you have been washed, you have been sanctified, you have been justified in the name of the Lord Jesus Christ and by the Spirit of our God.'

Augustine, speaking of our Lord Jesus' believing people, his 'bride,' commented, 'He loved her foul, that he might make her fair.' How many of us have cause to be grateful for the truth behind that quote! In John Newton's words, 'Amazing grace, how sweet the sound that saved a wretch like me . . .'

The unwelcome guest thrown out
What can we learn from the picture of the man who presumed on the goodness of the king and took a place at the banquet without having on a wedding garment?

Jesus said to Israel's religious leaders on an earlier occasion, quoting from Isaiah, 'This people honours me with their lips, but their heart is far from me; in vain do they worship me, teaching as doctrines the commandments of men.' In place of teaching the truths of God's word; his commandments, warnings and promises, they were teaching the current opinions of the time. It would be a shocking question to ask, but would our Lord have to say that of some, even of many, of today's religious leaders?

Even more serious are Jesus' words at the conclusion of the Sermon on the Mount. He warned that despite awesome miracles and years of public ministry, there would be those to whom he, as Lord and Judge, will have to say, 'I never knew you; depart from me . . .' Able and self-confident as they were, they would be 'cast out'.

We are in no position to judge who are truly the Lord God's people, and who are simply present among his people. Only the King can – and will – do that. It is the Lord God who searches the heart. He alone knows the secrets of all hearts and 'looks on the heart'.

It is also the Lord God who freely supplies the 'robe of righteousness,' the 'garment of salvation'. A garment which is worn, not as an outward adornment but is the hidden and inward gift of a 'new spirit and a new heart', a life made a 'new creation'. It is the God-given gift of forgiveness and peace with God through the mediation of the Son of God and a life filled and renewed by the Holy Spirit of God. In Richard Trench's words, '. . . the whole adornment of the new and spiritual man.'

For us, the guest without the wedding garment stands as a warning of the possibility of exclusion from the kingdom of heaven with all its joys and privileges. Like the religious leaders to whom Jesus was speaking, full of confidence in our acceptance before God, we may discover too late that before the King of kings we are actually unacceptable. It is a call to examine our own hearts, to humble ourselves, to plead for our forgiveness and for the gift of the 'garment of salvation' which alone makes us acceptable before the Lord God and his Son. Only then will we be welcome at the 'marriage supper of the Lamb', the great heavenly banquet given in honour of the Son of God, pictured in the book of Revelation.

The parable stands as a warning to those of us who, in one way or another, presume on the goodness of God. We may, to our horror, find ourselves cast out to our endless sorrow and regret.

For many are called but few are chosen
The parable concludes with this challenging saying. It would not only apply to the guest without the wedding garment, but also to those who had earlier refused to take notice of the invitation and come to the king's feast. They had all been called – and yet not one of those invited guests were actually present at the marriage feast.

The Scripture records that, of the great number of the people of Israel who, under the hand of God, were led by Moses out of captivity in Egypt to the promised land, only two actually entered it. (Caleb and Joshua)

Under the judgeship of Gideon, of the 32,000 men of Israel called to fight the Midianite overlords, only 300 were chosen of God to accomplish the victory.

The people of Israel had so often been called by the prophets of God to return to the Lord their God; to trust him and to obey him – but so few did. The constant and sad refrain of the prophets is reflected in the words of Jesus concerning the people and religious leaders in Jerusalem, 'But you would not!' 'You were not willing!'

In our own day, the people of Israel, scattered throughout the countries of the world and gathered into their ancient land, have been called to be the people of God, a people of praise and a glory, a magnet of godliness – and yet so few of them are willing, in the Lord God's words to Solomon, to '. . . humble themselves, and pray and seek his face and turn from their ungodly ways . . .'

So, many are called, and yet so few are chosen.

In the Gentile west, is our own generation's response to the call of the gospel so very different?

Heavenly Father, this parable was not intended to be comfortable hearing for the chief priests and Pharisees of Jesus' day. By your grace, cause us to walk humbly before you, accepting the truth, corrections, and challenges of your holy word.

Questions for personal reflection or discussion

1. Should the parable of the guests invited to the king's wedding feast cause us to shudder for seemingly unbelieving, politically-manoeuvering Christian leaders in our own day?
2. 'But they paid no attention.' Could these words apply to ourselves: When we hear the gospel call of God's preachers? Feel the Holy Spirit's prompting to serve the Lord in a particular way? Are aware of the God-given impression that we should help, or give?
3. 'While the rest seized his servants, treated them shamefully and killed them.' Our Lord's apostles were despised and rejected, arrested,

imprisoned, and many of them were martyred. Has it been like this through the running centuries? Can it still be like this in our day?

4. And those servants went out into the roads and gathered all whom they found, both bad and good.' Are we always comfortable with those whom the Lord's servants gather into his church?

5. One guest appeared to regard his own clothes as perfectly adequate for the banquet. In what ways can we presume on the goodness of the Lord God?

6. Can we assume we will be just fine, when, in fact, we do not have the Lord's provided 'garment of salvation', his 'robe of righteousness'?

7. In what ways can we look ahead and so avoid endless regret; the endless cry of, '. . . if only we had . . .' when we stand before the Lord?

References

The parable of the great banquet – Luke 15:15-24

O, Jerusalem, Jerusalem, the city that kills – Matthew 23:37-39

Blessed is everyone who will eat bread in the kingdom – Luke 14:15

Treasury store of 'festal garments' – Genesis 45:22, 2 Kings 5:5, Judges 14:13

Roman Centurion's servant – Matthew 8:5-13

Abraham, Isaac, and Jacob in the kingdom – Matthew 8:10.-12

Philip in Samaria – Acts 8:4-6

Peter preaching in Cornelius' house – Acts 10:30-43

Paul in Thessalonica – Acts 17:1-11 and Berea – Acts 17:10-12

The parable of the narrow door – Luke 13:27-30

Did not recognise the day of their visitation – Luke 19:44

You refuse to come to me that you may have life – John 5:39-40

You have been washed, sanctified, justified – 1 Corinthians 6:9-11

Teaching as doctrines the commandments of men – Matthew 15:8-9 and Isaiah 29:13

I never knew you; depart from me – Matthew 7:23

It is the Lord God who searches the heart – 1 Chronicles 28:9.

Looks on the heart – 1 Samuel 16:7

The 'robe of righteousness,' the 'garment of salvation' – Isaiah 61:10

A new spirit and a new heart – Ezekiel 11:19-20 and 36:26

A life made a new creation – 2 Corinthians 5:17 and Galatians 6:15

The marriage supper of the Lamb – Revelation 19:6-9

Only two entered the promised land – Numbers 14:22-24 and 30-31.

Of the 32,000, only 300 were chosen of God – Judges 7:1-8

'But you would not', or 'you were not willing' – Luke 13 34-35

Humble themselves and pray– 2 Chronicles 7:14

Many are called but few are chosen – Matthew 22:14

The Wise and the Foolish Virgins

"Then the kingdom of heaven will be like ten virgins who took their lamps and went to meet the bridegroom. Five of them were foolish, and five were wise. For when the foolish took their lamps, they took no oil with them, but the wise took flasks of oil with their lamps. As the bridegroom was delayed, they became drowsy and slept. But at midnight there was a cry, 'Here is the bridegroom! Come out to meet him.' Then all those virgins rose and trimmed their lamps. And the foolish said to the wise, 'Give us some of your oil, for our lamps are going out.' But the wise answered, saying, 'Since there will not be enough for us and for you, go rather to the dealers and buy for yourselves.' And while they were going to buy, the bridegroom came, and those who were ready went in with him to the marriage feast, and the door was shut. Afterwards the other virgins came also, saying, 'Lord, lord, open to us.' But he answered, 'Truly I say to you, I do not know you.' Watch therefore, for you know neither the day nor the hour.

Matthew 25:1-13 English Standard Version

The wise and the foolish virgins

The setting of the parable
Jesus had left the temple after a series of very strong exchanges with the Israel's most senior religious leaders; the chief priests, Pharisees and elders. Our Lord was now speaking privately to his disciples and preparing them for his leaving them.

Matthew records that the disciples had commented on the magnificence of the temple, but Jesus spoke of its future total destruction, 'not one stone left on another'. This caused the disciples to ask him, "Tell us, when will these things be, and what will be the sign of your coming and of the close of the age?" (Matthew 24:2-3) In reply, Jesus warned them of the very hard times they would face and of the fall of Jerusalem. He told them the parable of the fig tree, and of the signs to notice as his return, 'the coming of the Son of Man', drew nearer (Matthew 24:32-33).

Our Lord taught the disciples to be faithfully about his business and watchful for his return by a series of three parables. Finally, he gave them a glimpse of the judgement to come, as he told them the parable of the separation of the sheep and the goats (Matthew 25:31-34).

The first was the parable of the faithful and unfaithful servants and was explored in its fuller form as recorded in the gospel of Luke (Luke 12:41-48). It was a challenge to the whole group of disciples, and those who would follow them, to be faithful servants, playing their part in the whole 'household of God'. It was – and still is – a communal call to be faithful.

The parable of the wise and the foolish virgins, which follows it, is a challenge to be individually prepared for his return. Although his return was certain, yet its timing was completely unknown. It could have been very soon, or it could be at a far more distant time than the disciples imagined. Jesus gave the parable as a warning to them, and to each one of us, to be prepared for this.

The third parable in the series, the parable of the talents (Matthew 25:14-30), was a challenge to each individual disciple to play their part in building up the kingdom of God. Disciples in every age are to be employed in the Lord's business. It is a call to use well the gifts and abilities, wisdom and acquired knowledge with which we have been entrusted. The central message of the parable is very similar to the teaching of the parable of the pounds, or minas, found in the gospel of Luke (Luke 19:11-27).

The parable of the wise and the foolish virgins

The wedding scene Jesus pictured would immediately be recognised by his hearers. It was the familiar and homely scene of a typical young couple becoming married within the culture of those days.

There are many details not told us and commentators have wrestled with difficulties and unanswered questions in almost every sentence. However, at its simplest the order of the ceremonies seems to have been: on the appointed day, the bridegroom went to bring his bride from her father's house to the new home he had prepared. As there were no clocks or watches, the timing was simply, when all was ready and the bridegroom arrived to collect, first these young women, and then the bride herself. By custom this was some time in the evening and explains why lighted lamps or torches were needed. Together, they formed a brightly lit procession that made its way to the new home and to the place where the wedding festivities for the couple and their invited guests would take place.

In the parable, when the moment arrived, the young women took their lamps and prepared to meet the bridegroom. There were ten in all. Five of them were wise. Recognising that the wait for the groom might be very long, they had brought their lamps and a flask of oil to top them up. Five others did not show that forethought and were found to have been very foolish in not doing so.

The foolish virgins asked for some oil as their lamps were failing, but the wise virgins were unwilling share the oil they had brought, 'Since there will not be enough for us and for you, go rather to the dealers and buy for yourselves.' There was no animosity between the two groups. They would simply need the oil for their own lamps.

The bridegroom did not call for his bride until midnight, or as the Greek says, 'in the middle of the night'. Some time later, in the early hours of the morning, the foolish virgins – having obtained a fresh supply of oil for their lamps and missed the wedding procession – arrived at the place where the festivities were taking place. But by then, because of the risk of thieves and other unwelcome intruders, the door was securely fastened, and people unknown to the householder were firmly kept out.

The ten young women all had a desire to meet the bridegroom and accompany him to the wedding feast. They were all invited guests, and yet only five were eventually admitted. The others, through lack of preparedness for the long wait, were finally shut out.

The significance of the parable for the listening disciples
The Lord Jesus was continuing with a theme he had been following. It was the theme of being constantly ready for his certain return, even though the timing of it was completely unknown. In the previous chapter Matthew records that Jesus said to the disciples, "Therefore you also must be ready, for the Son of Man is coming at a time you do not expect" (Matthew 24:44). As he concluded this parable, Jesus said to the disciples, "Watch therefore, for you know neither the day nor the hour." (Matthew 25:13)

Our Lord was his own interpreter and so the parable of the ten virgins is a parable calling for preparation for, and perseverance throughout a long wait. There will come a time when it will be too late to get ready, and those found to be unprepared will be shut out. The door will be closed.

Jesus was calling the disciples to be watchful and, despite long delay, to live in a constant state of readiness for his return. The parable challenged them to think ahead and be prepared for this. As it applied to the disciples, so it would apply to those who came to faith through their witness and ministry. It is clear that the Lord Jesus was, and still is, looking for 'a people prepared' for his return.

As the rest of the New Testament makes clear, the disciples took note of this and almost everything preached, or written, was done in the light of the Lord's return.

For example, the apostle John in his first letter writes, 'Beloved, we are God's children now, and what we will be has not yet appeared; but we know that when he appears we shall be like him, because we shall see him as he is. And everyone who thus hopes in him purifies himself as he is pure.'

In the letter to the Thessalonians, which is thought to be the earliest of the New Testament letters, the apostle Paul wrote, ' . . .you turned to God from idols to serve the living and true God, and to wait for his Son from heaven, whom he raised from the dead, Jesus who delivers us from the wrath to come,' and, '. . . so that he may establish your hearts blameless in holiness before our God and Father, at the coming of our Lord Jesus with all his saints.'

Concluding the letter, he wrote, 'Now may the God of peace himself sanctify you completely, and may your whole spirit and soul and body be kept blameless at the coming of our Lord Jesus Christ. He who calls you is faithful; he will surely do it.'

Teaching about the Lord's Supper in his letter to the Corinthians, Paul wrote, 'For as often as you eat this bread and drink the cup, you proclaim the Lord's death until he comes.'

The significance of the parable for ourselves in our day
Constant readiness is our Lord's consistent command and instruction to those who are his people. Like the virgins awaiting the arrival of the bridegroom – despite the seeming delay – we need to constantly keep our eye on our Lord's return in great glory as Lord and Judge. All we do should be in the light of this and in preparation for it, so that we ourselves, and those around us, might be found on that great and yet terrifying day, a people prepared; a people about our Father's business and ready for the return of his glorious Son.

It is very easy to be enthusiastic and alert when we first learn of this, but to grow weary, spiritually sleepy and distracted by the busyness of life as time passes. Believers may live their lives and be 'gathered to their fathers' by death, before the Lord, the Bridegroom, comes – as each generation before our own has been. And yet, each generation is called to live in watchful anticipation of our Lord's sudden arrival.

Some practical steps
In order to keep his arrival in focus in all we say and do, we would do well to keep watch on the following:

The signs of the times in which we live – lest, like the slumbering virgins waiting for the bridegroom, when he suddenly arrives, we are caught drowsy, napping or even fast asleep.

Our hearts – lest, because of the long delay, they grow cold and disinterested.

Our minds – lest they be swept along by the world, which will constantly ask, "Where is the promise of his coming?" and dismiss it as 'a load of nonsense,' an 'idle tale'.

The company we keep – it is hard to stand firm when our close associates scoff.

The busy-ness of our lives, our leisure pursuits and our interests, lest we fail to be fruitful before the Lord. We need to be looking to the harvest, as the parable of the sower reminds us.

The state of the church – lest we fall into 'sleepy, comfortable Christianity'. Are our local church leaders calling us to be alert and watchful, are they helping us to be a people prepared for the Lord's return? Are they enabling and encouraging us to 'be about our Father's business?' Or is it a church which will gradually deflect us from such thinking, and lead us to be like some of those waiting for the bridegroom, drowsy or asleep, and totally unprepared? Does it offer Christianity in accord with our Lord's teaching, or are we simply encouraged to enjoy one another's company in the context of 'aesthetically pleasing services', 'well crafted services', 'entertaining services' or 'very comforting services'?

Links with other Scriptures and their possible spiritual significance

At midnight there was a cry, 'Here is the bridegroom! Could this, as Richard Trench suggests, picture the voice of archangel and trump of God? 'The heavenly bridegroom leading home his bride, the true people of God, to the glory of heaven which he has prepared for them?'

Trimmed their lamps Only when the bridegroom arrived did the foolish discover their error – and us? On what foundation does our hope of heaven depend, will it be found wanting at the last? "Please, give me some of your faith." We cannot ask those around us for that! We live and die according to our own preparation, our own obedient faith in the Son of God – or our lack of it. Even if our Grandma was very godly, or our Uncle a Bishop, other people's faith cannot carry us through death's gloomy portal to the heavenly banquet; the wedding feast of the Son of God.

Lord, lord, open to us Here is a sincere and earnest prayer, and yet it was offered too late. He never knew them. The good shepherd knows his sheep and is known of them; they alone walk closely with him, and to them he will open and welcome into his fold. (John 10:3-4, 14, 27-28)

The door is now shut The door through which tax gatherers and sinners enter. The door though which his sheep pass in and out and find pasture. The door, the great 'I am,' the Son of God, Lord Jesus himself. However, he is also the narrow door that will be closed. The door through which east and west come and sit down with Abraham, and yet the door that many, like the religious leaders of Jesus' day, will find, to their horror, closed against them, with themselves excluded. As the Scripture declares, 'Now is the day of salvation'. The days of grace will end and the door will be closed. (John 10:9, 10:36-38, 8:58, 2 Corinthians 6:2, Luke 13:24-29)

Watch therefore, for you do not know The five foolish virgins were so close to joining the bridal procession to the banquet, and yet . . .

Hence the solemnity of these words from our Lord's lips. While we do not know the timing, as Archbishop Trench notes, '. . . the only way to be ready on that day is to be ready on every day.' What a solemn warning – unreadiness on that day is unreadiness for ever.

Carved in stone in an ancient church for all to read is the warning, 'Be ye also ready for at such a time as ye think not, the Son of Man cometh.' (Matthew 24:44)

Heavenly Father, many centuries have passed since these words were spoken and we can easily grow cold, drowsy and anything but alert and watchful for your return, or even, as many do, dismiss it or reduce it to a fairy tale wish. By your grace help us to take very seriously this parable and actively 'live by faith in the Son of God who loved us and gave himself for us.' And so be found ready for the sudden, terrifying and glorious arrival of your Son as rightful Lord, King and Judge of us all.

Questions for personal reflection or discussion

1. Are you reminded of it often, or is it something of a surprise to you to learn of this serious call of our Lord to be prepared and ready for his return?

2. Each generation is called to live in watchful anticipation of our Lord's sudden arrival. Does this apply to those of us in a comfortable, settled western country? Are there signs it could be sooner than we think?

3. In what ways can we be a people prepared, a people about our Father's business and ready for the return of his glorious Son?

4. Do we need to keep a watch on:

– Our minds – lest they be swept along by the world, which will constantly ask, "Where is the promise of his coming?" and dismiss it as 'a load of nonsense,' an 'idle tale'. Do we hear such thinking from

THE WISE AND THE FOOLISH VIRGINS · 149

our TVs, computers and media personalities? How can we encourage one another to hold fast?

– The company we keep – how hard is it to stand firm when our close associates scoff?

– The busy-ness of our lives, our leisure pursuits and our interests – lest we fail to be fruitful before the Lord. Do we look to the harvest time, as the parable of the sower reminds us to?

– The state of the church – lest we fall into 'sleepy, comfortable Christianity.' Are our local church leaders calling us to be alert and watchful, are they helping us to be a people prepared for the Lord's return? Are they enabling and encouraging us to 'be about our Father's business'?

5. Is it very easy to be enthusiastic and alert when we first hear the gospel message to repent and believe, to 'take up our cross and follow', to seek to be fruitful before the Lord, to be alert and ready for his return – but to grow weary, spiritually sleepy and distracted by the busy-ness of life as time passes and we grow older? How can we help one another?

6. Only when the bridegroom arrived did the foolish virgins discover their error – and us? On what foundation does our hope of heaven depend, will it be found wanting at the last?

References

Not one stone left on another – Matthew 24:2
Son of Man is coming at a time you do not expect – Matthew 24:44
When he appears we shall be like him – 1 John 3:2-3
To wait for his Son from heaven – 1 Thessalonians 1:9-10
Establish your hearts blameless – 1 Thessalonians 3:13.
Blameless at the coming of our Lord Jesus Christ – 1 Thessalonians 5:23-24
Proclaim the Lord's death until he comes – 1 Corinthians 11:26
Where is the promise of his coming? – 2 Peter 3:3-4

An idle tale – Luke 24:11

When our close associates scoff – 2 Peter 3:3-4

The parable of the sower – Mark 4:1-20

The voice of archangel – 1Thessalonians 4:16

Obedient belief on the Son of God – or our lack of it – John 3:16

The door through which tax gatherers and sinners enter – Matthew 21:31-32

The door though which his sheep pass in and out and find pasture – John 10:7-9

The door, the great 'I am,' the Son of God, Lord Jesus himself – John 10:7

The narrow door that will be closed – Luke 13:24-30

East and west come and sit down with Abraham – Luke 13:28-30

Now is the day of salvation – 2 Corinthians 6:2

Be ye also ready for at such a time as ye think not, the Son of Man cometh – Matthew 24:44

Live by faith in the Son of God who loved us – Galatians 2:20

Take up our cross and follow – Matthew 10:38

The Talents

Watch therefore, for you know neither the day nor the hour. For it will be like a man going on a journey, who called his servants and entrusted to them his property. To one he gave five talents, to another two, to another one, to each according to his ability. Then he went away. He who had received the five talents went at once and traded with them, and he made five talents more. So also he who had the two talents made two talents more. But he who had received the one talent went and dug in the ground and hid his master's money. Now after a long time the master of those servants came and settled accounts with them. And he who had received the five talents came forward, bringing five talents more, saying, 'Master, you delivered to me five talents; here I have made five talents more.' His master said to him, 'Well done good and faithful servant. You have been faithful over little, I will set you over much. Enter into the joy of your master.' And he also who had the two talents came forward saying, 'Master, you delivered to me two talents; here, I have made two talents more.' His master said to him, 'Well done good and faithful servant. You have been faithful over little, I will set you over much. Enter into the joy of your master.' He also who had received the one talent came forward saying, 'Master, I knew you to be a hard man, reaping where you did not sow, and gathering where you scattered no seed, so I was afraid, and went and hid your talent in the ground. Here you have what is yours.' But his master answered him, 'You wicked and slothful servant! You knew that I reap where I have not sowed and gather where I scattered no seed? Then you ought to have invested my money with the bankers, and at my coming I should have received what was my own with interest. So take the talent from him and give it to the one who has the ten talents. For to everyone who has, more will be given, and he will have an abundance. But from the one who has not, even what he has will be taken away. And cast the worthless servant into the outer darkness. In that place there will be weeping and gnashing of teeth.

Matthew 25:13-30 English Standard Version

The Parable of the Talents

The setting of the parable
Jesus was continuing to teach his disciples about being ready for his return. The parable follows his call to constant watchfulness for his return, his warning to be his faithful servants about their Master's business, and the warning given to them by way of the parable of the ten virgins, only five of whom had made careful preparation and were found to be ready.

Immediately after telling them the parable of the ten virgins, the gospel records Jesus saying to the disciples, 'Watch therefore, for you know neither the day nor the hour. For it will be like a man going on a journey, who called his servants and entrusted to them his property. To one he gave five talents, to another two, to another one, to each according to his ability.'

The parable of the talents is one of the most widely known parables, and the word 'talent' has become part of the English language as we speak, for example, of 'a very talented young person' or of 'very talented musicians'.

A talent was originally a weight of precious metal. In the parable it was a weight of silver coins. The value of each talent the man gave his servants is debated, but could have been worth as much as twenty years' wages for a working man.

The parable's relationship with a similar parable
The parable of the talents has many similarities with the less well known parable of the pounds or minas recorded in the gospel of Luke.

Unlike the parable of the talents, in the parable of the pounds, the ten pounds were shared out equally between the servants; a single 'pound' being given to each servant. This parable was taught publicly to a wide crowd of hearers, including the disciples, after Jesus had passed through Jericho on his final journey up to Jerusalem.

The parable of the pounds had a strong and memorable local background. The picture of a nobleman going away to receive a kingdom would immediately be familiar to the people of Jericho, as that is exactly what their own ruler, Archelaus, had had to do. He had to go to Rome to request Caesar to grant him the delegated authority to rule. This was required of any military leader within the Roman Empire who hoped to become king of the area he had conquered or, as in Archelaus' case, had inherited. He was not granted the title 'king', but was given the authority to rule.

The parable of the pounds was given to correct a mistaken idea, firmly held by the disciples, the religious leaders and the people of Israel generally. As a conquered people, they yearned for the triumphant kingdom of God's Messiah to be fulfilled in a military and earthly way. The all-conquering Roman rulers would be thrown out and the nation of Israel restored to the power and glory of the days of David and Solomon.

By the parable of the pounds, Jesus was showing them that such thinking was an error and obscured the truth declared by the prophets that 'the Christ must suffer'. The nation of Israel was clinging on to what was merely a nationalistic dream. Jesus was truly their long promised Messiah – but he was the suffering servant of the Lord described by the prophet Isaiah, and he was actually on his way to Jerusalem and the cross. He would leave them, but after he had been raised from the dead and given the kingdom, he would return as triumphant king. On his return he would call to account his servants – and, just as Archelaus had done, also call to account those who refused to submit to him.

The parable of the talents

The parable of the talents is quite different, both in its setting and in its aim. It was shared privately with his disciples in the very last days of Jesus' ministry as he prepared to leave them. It was given to make clear to them the very great responsibility he was entrusting to them and to strongly encourage them be his faithful servants as they fulfilled that responsibility.

Jesus compared himself with a man entrusting his wealth into the hands of his servants, the Greek refers to them as his slaves. (Very much as Pharaoh entrusted the affairs and future well-being of Egypt into the hands of Joseph. Pharaoh made him 'prime minister', but he was still a slave, although an honoured one.)

The talents shared out according to ability

By genetic make-up, by the experiences of life and by the training we have received, we are all different. Some have greater natural ability or have more experience than others. Wisdom demands that the weightier responsibilities are entrusted to those most suited to bear them, rather than to those for whom such responsibilities might prove a crippling burden. The master of these servants recognised this, and so entrusted each servant with an appropriate amount of money with which to trade. Having put his affairs into the hands of his servants, the man took his journey.

On his return, 'after a long time', the master called each of his servants to give an account of their use of the talents he had given them. 'He who had received the five talents went at once and traded with them, and he made five talents more. So also he who had the two talents . . .' The first two servants had been diligent and busy in the pursuit of their master's business from the start. They could come before him with confidence, 'Look I have made . . .' They had each put their master's talents to good use on his behalf, and were commended for doing so.

The third servant failed to put his master's money to good use. He merely kept it safe. But his master had given the talent to him expecting him to trade with it. The master was looking for faithfulness over the little he had entrusted to this servant, just as much as for faithfulness in those servants to whom he had entrusted much.

Burying treasure to keep it relatively safe was common practice in uncertain days. But his master was looking, not just for its safe return, but for an increase in its value from its investment.

The servant's reasoning and excuses were an attempt to turn the blame from himself to his master, 'a hard man', or 'a severe man'. And, 'I was afraid.' Was he afraid because he would be attempting to trade with this relatively small sum, and might lose all or some of it? If that should happen, might he incur the wrath of this 'hard' master, who might even demand that he make up the loss personally?

Quoting the servant's own words, his master condemns him for his idleness. As the servant recognised that his master was severe, at the very least he should have put 'the silver pieces' – the Greek makes plain that is what they were – into the hands of the bankers and investors of the day. His master would then have received his money, together with interest. The servant had failed in his commission from his master to use the talent well.

As a result, the money was taken from him and given to the first servant who could be trusted to make good use of it. As Jesus said, 'For to everyone who has more will be given, and he will have an abundance. But from the one who has not, even what he has will be taken away. And cast the worthless servant into the outer darkness. In that place there will be weeping and gnashing of teeth.'

Weeping and gnashing of teeth

The servant was taken and put out. He had lost his job, his income, and possibly the home in which he was living, if that was provided by the master. Perhaps with his family, he was out on the street weeping and gnashing his teeth in regret of his lack of forethought, boldness and faithful activity for his master. He could not be commended to another employer, and to his endless regret he had now to beg or begin as the lowest day worker, scraping a living to support himself and such family as depended on him. Darkness, indeed, and gnashing of teeth. If the unfaithful servant was in fact a slave, his fate may have been even more terrible.

If the picture our Lord painted is that bad at a human level, what must it be, to be found unfaithful before the Son of Man? This is a most solemn parable and warning.

The application of the parable to the disciples
Jesus was preparing the disciples for his leaving them 'for a long time'. Before he left, he was going to commit into their hands the founding and building of his church on earth.

After his resurrection, Jesus commissioned his disciples to 'go into all the world and proclaim the gospel.' To 'make disciples of all nations,' and then to undertake the ongoing responsibility of teaching them all he had commanded them. Finally, as he said to Peter, to continue to 'feed his sheep and tend his flock' – until his return.

The disciples each had their own natural gifts, abilities, and weaknesses. However, together with God the Father, Jesus promised that he would send the enabling of the Holy Spirit for the work, and he gave them his promise to be 'with them to the end of the age,' and his return.

That the disciples slowly came to understand the great commission their Lord was putting into their hands, is plain from the rest of the New Testament. In the Acts of the Apostles we read of Peter and John, and later of Paul, actively about their Master's business, and their letters reflect the faithful care and attention they gave as they 'tended' the little flocks of their Lord's people scattered throughout the Roman Empire.

Not only did the apostles work diligently themselves, they also trained and passed on the charge to faithful believers who were able to 'tend the flock,' and so carry forward the task. The existence of groups of believing people throughout the world in our day bears witness to their faithfulness.

The application of the parable to ourselves in our day
'After a long time.' Could this phrase be a hint that our Lord's return would be long delayed and not as soon as it seems the disciples and some early believers came to expect?

The parable of the ten virgins reflects our need to take practical steps to keep our heart and mind close to our Lord, and so be prepared for his return. The parable of the talents shows us in a very practical way that, as we are able, and no matter how small the opportunities given to us, we are called to be diligently about our Master's business, seeking to honour him and further his interests.

We use the word 'talent' of all our skills and abilities, no matter what they are, or how we choose to use them. However, in the parable, Jesus was giving the disciples a picture of gifts and abilities he would give them to use on his behalf. The talents they would be given were to be used as they were about his business; the preaching of his gospel, the making and building up of his disciples, and the tending of the churches that would be formed as a result of their faithful work.

He . . . went at once and traded with them
The two first servants showed diligence and had success, they were faithful and single-minded and busy in their master's service from the first day onwards.

All through the centuries, believers who have come to faith through the witness of the apostles and their successors, have carried forward this same responsibility of proclaiming the gospel, building up and teaching fellow disciples and playing a part among the people of God. The whole picture of the kingdom of God as it now is on earth is like a world-wide, centuries-long relay race. One generation after the next is entrusted with the 'gospel baton' to faithfully hand on to the next generation. If we are unfaithful and 'bury our talent', or 'bury the gospel' with our own ideas and the current opinions of the age in which we live, true biblical believers will die out within a generation or two – as seems to be currently happening throughout the English-speaking world.

What can we learn from the third servant?
Jesus constantly taught in parables, and so there is a link with the previous parable of the virgins. We can assume, like the five foolish virgins awaiting the bridegroom, that the Lord will be returning very soon and so we need not trouble ourselves too much with proper care and preparation.

Or we can be like this third servant, too fearful, too self-effacing and hesitant, seeing only the difficulties, rather than the God-given opportunities to further his kingdom? These parables give us the two equal and opposite pitfalls into either one of which we may find ourselves inclined to tumble.

In the parable, Jesus emphasised the failure and the fate of the third servant. There is a strong warning in this for us. It is not only for those who squander their God-given talent or talents on their own concerns and pleasure, as the prodigal son did with his father's money. It is also for those who, being called and equipped for a sphere of responsibility in the kingdom of God, choose rather to put that calling to one side; to 'bury it'. We can certainly do so by filling our life with our own personal pursuits and interests. But like the third servant, we can also 'bury it' by being 'afraid', choosing to live a quiet life and so leaving the opportunity unfulfilled. This could be due to a misplaced humility, but it leaves 'buried' the opportunity to love and serve the Lord God by serving, encouraging and building up his people. The third servant could restore the buried talent, but we cannot restore lost opportunities of usefulness before our heavenly Father. Drawing attention to this danger, both John Owen and Richard Trench call us to bear in mind that 'we are called to serve our generation according the will of God.'

There will be many failings in any work we undertake for the Lord, but it is a mistake to think of him, as this servant did, as a hard and unforgiving task-master, of whom one might reasonably 'be afraid'.

Like the first two servants, if we faithfully 'trade' with the 'talent' or 'talents' the Master has entrusted to us, we will discover the truth of our Lord's words, 'Take my yoke upon you, and learn from me, for I am gentle and lowly in heart, and you will find rest for your souls.' 'Rest', not the rest of idleness, but the fulfilment and peace of mind that comes from undertaking a task for which we were created and which exactly fits our temperament and God-given abilities. By inviting us to trade with our 'talents', our heavenly Father is encouraging us to grow in ability and usefulness to the One 'whose service is perfect freedom.'

As a Christian minister, I confess to long putting off a willingness to take and put on that 'yoke'. Even now, I am all but overwhelmed by the patience, kindness and mercy of the Lord God with such a stubborn and unwilling servant.

Because of his neglect of it, the talent was taken from the unfaithful servant and given to the first servant. As a consequence of his failure to use it, the third servant lost the opportunity to trade with it. God-given opportunities for service will pass. As the unfaithful servant found, the Lord God is well able to choose others to take our place in his service.

The days of grace and mercy will not be ended until the Lord's return and the final calling to account. Until then, there is opportunity to turn and amend our neglectful ways; to 'dig up our talent' and live to obey and honour him. The servant had such an opportunity all the time his master was away – but he left it too late.

For the disciples to whom it was first told, and to us in our day, the parable stands as an encouragement and as a warning. A warning to beware of the fate of the useless servant, and an encouragement to keep before us a longing to hear from our Lord's lips some echo of the words spoken to the first two faithful servants, 'Well done good and faithful servant . . . enter into the joy of your Lord.'

Heavenly Father we know something of this parable so well, it is in our everyday language. Despite its familiarity, please help us not to miss its very serious challenge to use the days you give us in a way that brings honour to your holy name, reaches out to others and builds up our fellow believers.

Questions for reflection or group discussion

1. The parable of the talents shows us in a very practical way, that as we are able, and no matter how small the opportunities given to us, we are called to be diligently about our Master's business, seeking to honour him and further his interests. Does this mean we must all become preachers, church planters , pastors and ministers, or can we be equally called and equipped to be salt and light for him at every level in society?

2. The whole picture of the kingdom of God, as it now is on earth, is like a world-wide, centuries-long relay race. One generation after the next is entrusted with the 'gospel baton' to faithfully hand on to the next generation. How are we doing and how can we better play our part?

3. If we are unfaithful, 'bury our talent', or 'bury the gospel' with our own ideas and the current opinions of the age in which we live, true biblical believers will die out within a generation or two – as seems to be currently happening throughout the English-speaking world. Should this be a matter of grave concern to us? Could this be a wake-up call to Christian ministers? Should it drive us to our knees to pray for the Holy Spirit to send a revival? What part can we play?

4. Can we sometimes be like the third servant, too fearful, too self-effacing and hesitant, seeing only the difficulties, rather than the God-

given opportunities to further his kingdom? Do we need to encourage one another to boldly embrace opportunities to serve the Lord?

5. If we faithfully 'trade' with the 'talent' the Master has entrusted to us, we will discover. . . the fulfilment and the easiness that comes from undertaking a task for which we were created and which exactly fits our temperament and God-given abilities. How true is that in our experience, or in the experience of someone we know?

6. The days of grace and mercy will not be ended until the Lord's return and the final calling to account. Until then, there is opportunity to turn and amend our neglectful ways; to 'dig up our talent' and live to obey and honour him. Is there a solemn challenge here?

7. Our talents may be few and our circumstances may greatly limit us, but would it be good from time to time to ask, 'Could I be better using the talents the Lord has entrusted to me for his glory?'

References

Parable of the pounds – Luke 19:11-27
The days of David and Solomon – Acts 1:6
The Christ must suffer – Luke 24:25-27
The suffering servant of the Lord – Isaiah 53:4-6
Joseph a slave of Pharoh – Genesis 41:33-46
Go into all the world and proclaim the gospel – Mark 16:15
Make disciples of all nations – Matthew 28:19-20
Feeding his sheep and tending his flock – John 21:15-17
With them to the end of the age – Matthew 28:20
Faithful believers who were able to 'tend the flock – 1Peter 5:1-4
The prodigal son – Luke 15:11-13
You will find rest for your souls – Matthew 11:29
(Whose service is perfect freedom – A phrase from the Collect for Peace in Morning Prayer, Book of Common Prayer)

The Sheep and the Goats

"When the Son of Man comes in his glory, and all the angels with him, then he will sit on his glorious throne. Before him will be gathered all the nations, and he will separate the people one from another as a shepherd separates the sheep from the goats. And he will place the sheep on his right, but the goats on his left. Then the King will say to those on his right, 'Come, you who are blessed by my Father, inherit the kingdom prepared for you from the foundation of the world. For I was hungry and you gave me food, I was thirsty and you gave me drink, I was a stranger and you welcomed me, I was naked and you clothed me, I was sick and you visited me, I was in prison and you came to me.' Then the righteous will answer him, saying, Lord, when did we see you hungry and feed you, or thirsty and give you drink? And when did we see you a stranger and welcome you, or naked and clothe you? And when did we see you sick or in prison and visit you?' And the King will answer them, 'Truly, I say to you, as you did it to the least of these my brothers, you did it to me.'

Then he will say to those on his left, 'Depart from me you cursed, into the eternal fire prepared for the devil and his angels. For I was hungry and you gave me no food, I was thirsty and you gave me no drink, I was a stranger and you did not welcome me, naked and you did not clothe me, sick and in prison and you did not visit me.' Then they also will answer, saying, 'Lord, when did we see you hungry or thirsty or a stranger or naked or sick or in prison, and did not minister to you?' Then he will answer them saying, 'Truly, I say to you, as you did not do it to one of the least of these, you did not do it to me.' And these will go away into eternal punishment, but the righteous into eternal life."

Matthew 25:31-46 English Standard Version

When Jesus had finished all these sayings, he said to his disciples, "You know that after two days the Passover is coming, and the Son of Man will be delivered up to be crucified."

Then the chief priests and the elders of the people gathered in the palace of the high priest whose name was Caiaphas, and plotted together in order to arrest Jesus by stealth and kill him. But they said, "Not during the feast, lest there be an uproar among the people."

Matthew 26:1-5 English Standard Version

The Sheep and the Goats

Introduction
"Oh," she said, "What is the matter with goats? I keep them myself and love their milk." There is clearly nothing the matter with goats! They are very hardy and valuable animals, particularly in hilly and semi-arid countryside, as much of the land of Israel is. Their wool can be woven into clothing and their milk and meat provide food.

The Lord was not downgrading goats, but simply showing, by a picture, what would have been very familiar to his hearers, that sheep and goats are different and, although they were often shepherded together in the open country, they were separated by the shepherd and kept in different folds at night. Sheep, especially the ewes, are quiet and obedient – most of the time! They know and will hear the voice of the shepherd and are contented when the shepherd is with them to lead them, feed them and protect them. Goats, on the other hand, are far more independent and can be fierce and quarrelsome. Ezekiel, speaking of shepherding the people of Israel, used the picture of the need to separate unruly sheep, rams and he-goats.

The setting of the parable
Although this passage is often treated as if it stood alone, the gospel of Matthew records the parable of the sheep and the goats as the final

parable of a series. John Calvin sees it as being continuous with the preceding parables, and the conclusion of Jesus' preparation of the disciples for a long time to elapse before his return.

The whole series of parables is recorded in Matthew chapters 24 and 25, and began with Jesus explaining to the disciples that despite their awe of the impressive temple that king Herod had built, "...there will not be left here one stone upon another that will not be thrown down."

As he sat on the Mount of Olives, the disciples came to him privately, saying, "Tell us, when these things will be, and what will be the sign of your coming, and of the close of the age?"

In answer to that question, Jesus gave a prophetic overview of the near and distant future – concluding with his own return. He spoke of the timing of the return of the 'Son of Man' by way of the parable of the budding fig tree.

In the series of parables that followed, Jesus taught his disciples how he would have them live during the time between his leaving them and his return in power and great glory.

He told them that his return would be sudden and unexpected, so he challenged the disciples to be constantly ready, like faithful servants awaiting the return of their master. "Therefore, you also must be ready, for the Son of Man is coming at an hour you do not expect."

He challenged them to be prepared for a possible very long wait. They were to be like the wise virgins awaiting the bridegroom who brought with them not only their lamps but a flask of spare oil in case the bridegroom was delayed. "Watch therefore, for you know neither the day nor the hour."

He challenged them to use well all he had entrusted to them "for it will be like a man going on a journey, who called his servants and entrusted to them his property."

Finally, he warned them, "When the Son of Man comes in his glory, and all the angels with him, then he will sit on his glorious throne.

Before him will be gathered all the nations, and he will separate the people one from another as a shepherd separates the sheep from the goats."

By the whole series of parables, Jesus was preparing his disciples for his leaving them, showing them how he would have them live during his absence, and how they were to live in readiness for his return.

The parable of the sheep and the goats is Jesus' final piece of teaching before his arrest and crucifixion. It is a gathering together of all that Jesus had taught his disciples, as they overlooked Jerusalem from the slopes of the Mount of Olives.

When Jesus had finished all these sayings, he said to his disciples. "You know that after two days the Passover is coming, and the Son of Man will be delivered up to be crucified."

Were the religious leaders aware of these parables and their implications? We are not told, but Matthew gives a hint that they may have been. If so, they would have been all the more incensed because they were a very clear statement of who he, Jesus, truly is – the Lord God's anointed Son, the Messiah, the long awaited Christ, the King and ultimate Judge. They could not bear to hear, let alone tolerate such a claim.

Whether the religious leaders were made aware of these particular parables or not, they had drawn their own conclusion from the implications of Jesus' teaching as a whole and, 'were plotting together in order to arrest Jesus by stealth and kill him.'

The parable of the sheep and the goats itself
The gospel of Matthew is the gospel of the King from beginning to end. After the birth of Jesus, the gospel begins with the enquiry, 'Where is he who has been born king of the Jews?' Throughout his life, our Lord's teaching, as it is recorded in Matthew's gospel, was about how to enter, and how life should be lived, as a citizen of the

'kingdom of heaven'. Jesus lived a very simple life among the ordinary people, and yet as he finally rode on a humble donkey into Jerusalem, Matthew records, 'this took place to fulful what was spoken by the prophet, saying, "Say to the daughter of Zion, 'Behold your king is coming to you, humble, and mounted on a donkey . . ..'"

The disciples, and those who would succeed them, were to be entrusted with the task of calling out a people throughout all the nations of the earth who will be ready for his return. For when he does return, he will do so no longer as the humble Son of Man they had known but in great glory as King and Judge, with ministering angels as his attendants.

The significance of the parable of the sheep and the goats
'When the Son of Man comes in his glory, and all the angels with him, then he will sit on his glorious throne. Before him will be gathered all the nations, and he will separate the people one from another as a shepherd separates the sheep from the goats. And he will place the sheep on his right, but the goats on his left.'

Jesus was showing the disciples – and us in our day – that on his glorious return there will be a separation, like a shepherd's separation of sheep and goats. As King and Judge, he will distinguish between and separate those who are truly his, from those who mistakenly assume they are his or who firmly reject him.

Although, like sheep and goats on hillside, we live alongside one another in this present age, there is a day coming when we will be separated. It would be like the separation of the shepherd's flocks, in that a clear distinction will be drawn, but, in the case of men and women, it will be terrible in its seriousness. 'Then he will answer [those he is separating from his own true people] saying, "Truly, I say to you, as you did not do it to one of the least of these, you did not do it to me." And these will go away into eternal punishment, but the righteous into eternal life.'

The distinguishing features of the Shepherd's true sheep
Matthew Henry points out that the returning King will not automatically set on his right people of status; the rich, the noble and those endowed with great intellect. He will by no means exclude them, but will select godly people; people who, whatever their status in life, had lived as his faithful and obedient servants.

'Then the King will say to those on his right, 'Come, you who are blessed by my Father, inherit the kingdom prepared for you from the foundation of the world. For I was hungry and you gave me food, I was thirsty and you gave me drink, I was a stranger and you welcomed me, I was naked and you clothed me, I was sick and you visited me, I was in prison and you came to me.'

Both John Calvin and Matthew Henry draw attention to a mistaken conclusion that we can draw if we read the parable and its teaching on its own, without reference to the setting. On the surface the verses seem to suggest that those who look after the needs of others, by helping and supporting them, will be approved by the King. By their good deeds, they will have come to deserve or merit a place on his right hand and so be destined for the joy of inheriting the kingdom prepared for them.

However, the Lord's teaching is quite the other way round. Our Lord was speaking to his disciples. He was speaking to those who, with the exception of Judas, loved him and longed to honour and obey him. To his believing disciples, Jesus was showing how obedience to his commandment, to love one another, might work out in practice. These are actions and kindnesses that demonstrate the love and the obedience to the Lord of his true believers. Such evidence of the genuineness of our love and obedient faith toward him are, as J. C. Ryle notes, 'written in heaven'.

Although it is not made clear within the verses of this parable, performing these acts of kindness is not a way of securing a place in the kingdom of heaven. They are almost unnoticed examples of the fruit of being a true member of it. In William Hendriksen's words concerning our Lord's true servants, 'Their good works are the fruit, not the root, of grace'.

The acts kindness our Lord drew to the attention of the disciples, are only very mistakenly understood to be 'a way of winning God's favour', and so securing a place at the King's right hand.

The King will draw a distinction between those who are truly his people, and those who are not. His people are known to him by the way they honour and obey him as they go about putting his commandments to love and forgive one another into practice. Jesus selects almost incidental actions that show a real love and concern for those who are his people. These actions are so 'insignificant' that they go unnoticed by those who habitually practise them.

'Then the righteous will answer him, saying, Lord, when did we see you hungry and feed you, or thirsty and give you drink? And when did we see you a stranger and welcome you, or naked and clothe you? And when did we see you sick or in prison and visit you?' And the King will answer them, 'Truly, I say to you, as you did it to the least of these my brothers, you did it to me.'

Why did Jesus pick out these particular signs of small and almost unnoticed personal faithfulness, rather than, for example, effective public ministry? On his return as King he will not say, 'Come, you who are blessed by my Father, inherit the kingdom prepared for you from the foundation of the world, for you have preached in my name, and done mighty works in my name.' He will not say that, because there will be those who could claim to have done these things – and yet who are total strangers to him.

Nor did he say these words because his true people, his 'sheep,' did not commit great failings – murder, adultery and theft, for example. The Pharisees could lay claim to near perfect lives before God in these respects, and yet their 'hearts were far from him'. They strictly kept the laws prohibiting such things. But, like their forebears, they totally neglected and even despised the 'flock of God' they were called to feed and care for.

With the exception of Judas, the disciples laid down their lives to 'feed the Lord's sheep and tend his lambs', putting into practice the sort of things Jesus listed.

The returning King chose these very small and all but unnoticed examples of personal care and concern for those he counted as his brothers. These were the little acts of love and care that mark the life of a true disciple, a life reflecting his teaching to love one another, care for one another and forgive one another.

The apostle Paul wrote, 'by love serve one another'. The little, easily forgotten acts of kindness that our Lord as returning King will notice, are acts doing just that. They were, just as Jesus taught, 'cups of cold water' given in his name.

'Truly, I say to you, as you did it to the least of these my brothers, you did it to me.'

Who are the people Jesus referred to as 'my brothers'? It has been suggested that Jesus was speaking of his disciples and of the reception that would be given to them as they proclaimed the gospel. The distinction would then be between those who welcomed both the message they proclaimed, and cared and supported them as the messengers of gospel truth, and those who did not.

If we widen that, it would apply to succeeding generations of those who proclaimed the gospel and faithfully taught 'all that Jesus had commanded'. The first of those might have been Philip who was invited to explain to the Ethiopian eunuch the passage of Scripture from the book of Isaiah, and who faithfully shared the gospel with him.

Then, at Philippi, Lydia believed the message of the apostle Paul, and welcomed him to her home. In later years, the apostle was well loved and cared for by the church in Philippi, who sent him gifts for his support and sent one of their members to visit and encourage him.

It was the gospel writer Luke, who joined the apostle Paul in Philippi, and who in later years stood by the apostle during his final time of imprisonment in Rome.

The definition of the Lord's faithful brothers and sisters would, logically, include those who faithfully proclaim the gospel and teach his commandments in our day. This would include faithful church leaders, Sunday school teachers, missionaries in this country and abroad, and those who welcome their gospel ministry, join them and assist them in any way they can.

The gospel of Mark records that, early in his ministry, the Lord Jesus gave a very wide definition of his true brothers and sisters. The definition would include all those who are faithful and obedient believers. '. . . they said to him, "Your mother and your brothers are outside, seeking you." And he answered them, "Who are my mother and my brothers?" And looking about him, he said, "Here are my mother and my brothers! Whoever does the will of God, he is my brother and sister and mother."

In conclusion:
The whole series of parables' relevance to us in our day
It would be easy to say, 'Yes, very interesting,' and then pass on, but that would be a mistake. Why? Because these parables and their teaching, first entrusted to the disciples on the Mount of Olives, are a challenge to us during the 'age of the church' as we await the return of the King.

We, in our turn, are still called to go and make disciples, still called to teach others all that Jesus commanded, still called to do all we can to create a people throughout the world prepared for the return of our mighty Lord and Saviour the King of kings. We are still called to be watching and waiting, individually making the most God-honouring use of the talents entrusted to us, and living the life of the kingdom here and now – habitually doing the acts of kindness, help, support and encouragement for our fellow believers that our Lord described in this final parable.

The whole series of parables is a challenge to us to live consistent and godly lives, both as individuals and as companies of the Lord's people. Our own lives and homes, and the communal lives of our churches and chapels are to be a foretaste of the 'kingdom of heaven'. We are called to be lights in this dark world, oases of godly refreshment in an arid and increasingly godless society. Our individual and our communal lives marked by 'kingdom of heaven living', here and now.

Living in the way Jesus described in this series of parables, we will not be caught by surprise or fall short when the Son of Man comes in his glory, and all the angels with him and, seated on his glorious throne, separates us as a shepherd separates the sheep from the goats.

Heavenly Father we thank you for this final parable from the Lord Jesus' lips before his crucifixion. Help us by your grace and the enabling of the Holy Spirit to be a people prepared for 'the return of the Son of Man'. Watching, waiting, faithful, thoughtful, making the best use of the talents and opportunities you give us, and from the heart humbly supporting and caring for the fellow members of your household; our brothers and sisters in the Lord.

Questions for reflection or group discussion

1. 'We in our turn are still called to go and make disciples, still called to teach others all that Jesus commanded, still called to do all we can to create a people throughout the earth prepared for the return of our mighty Lord and Saviour the King of kings.' How can we each actively play our part in this?

2. 'We are still called to be watching and waiting' for the King's return. How can we keep this aspect of the gospel message to the fore in our thinking and in our churches and chapels?

3. 'Living the life of the kingdom here and now, habitually doing the almost unnoticed little acts of kindness, help, support and encouragement of fellow believers our Lord described . . .' In what ways could we and our fellow Christians be more active in doing this?

4. 'Our own lives and homes, and that of our churches and chapels should be a foretaste of the 'kingdom of heaven'. We are called to be lights in this dark world, oases of godly refreshment in an arid and increasingly godless society. Our individual and our communal lives marked by 'kingdom of heaven living,' here and now. Not easy in the fallen world in which we live, but is this truly our aim, and how can we encourage and support one another?

5. 'Living in this way, we will not be caught by surprise by the certain yet sudden return of the King.' A truly terrifying and yet wonderful prospect. How can we help and encourage one another to be ready, and do all we can to help those around us to be ready?

References

Unruly sheep, rams and he-goats – Ezekiel 34:17-19.
In order to arrest Jesus by stealth and kill him – Matthew 26:3-5
He who has been born king of the Jews – Matthew 2:1-2
Say to the daughter of Zion, 'Behold your king . . . – Matthew 21:5, Zechariah 9:9
Mighty works in his name, yet strangers to him – Matthew 7:21-23
The Pharisees, 'whose hearts were far from him' – Matthew 15:8
Despised the 'flock of God' they were called to feed – Ezekiel 34:2-4
Feed the Lord's sheep and tend his lambs – John 21:15-17
Teaching to love one another – John 13:34-35
Forgive one another – Matthew 6:14-15
Serve one another – Mark 10:43-45

By love serve one another – Galatians 5:13
A cup of cold water given in his name – Matthew 10:40-42
Philip and the Ethiopian eunuch – Acts 8:27-35
At Philippi, Lydia welcomed and believed – Acts 16:14-15
The apostle cared for by the church in Philippi – Philippians 4:10-16
Luke alone stood by the apostle Paul in Rome – 2 Timothy 4:11
Who are my mother and my brothers? – Mark 3:32-35
When the Son of Man comes in his glory – Matthew 25:31-32

Footnote
There is debate among the commentators whether this account of the separation of the sheep and goats and its associated teaching is strictly a parable. It certainly is not a typical parable. It seems to begin as a parable but seamlessly moves to become direct and straightforward teaching.

Final Words

The Great Commission
At the conclusion of his gospel, Matthew records that after Jesus had been arrested, tried and put to death, he, the now risen Lord, met with the disciples and gave them these words of challenge and great encouragement:

Now the eleven disciples went to Galilee, to the mountain to which Jesus had directed them. And when the saw him they worshipped him, but some doubted. And Jesus said to them, "All authority in heaven and on earth has been given to me. Go therefore and make disciples of all nations, baptizing them in the name of the Father and of the Son and of the Holy Spirit, teaching them to observe all that I have commanded you. And behold, I am with you always, to the end of the age."

Matthew 28:16-20 English Standard Version

Principal Sources

Holy Bible English Standard Version, Containing the Old and New Testaments, Anglicised Edition. Collins, 2002.

William Barclay: *The Daily Study Bible, The Gospel of Matthew*. The Saint Andrew Press, Edinburgh, Eleventh Impression 1970. – William Barclay (1907-1978) was Professor of Divinity and Biblical Criticism at the University of Glasgow.

John Bunyan: *The Pilgrim's Progress*. Edited with an Introduction and Notes by Roger Sharrock. Penguin Books 1965. – John Bunyan, (1628-1688) 'The Tinker of Bedford', was a Puritan preacher and writer. For his persistent 'illegal' preaching, he spent some twelve years in prison. It was during this time that he began to write his most well known work *The Pilgrim's Progress*.

John Calvin: *Commentary on a Harmony of the Evangelists, Matthew, Mark, and Luke*. Translated from the original Latin, and collated with the Author's French version by the Rev. William Pringle. Wm. B. Eerdmans. – John Calvin (1509-64) was the great French reformer and theologian. He was forced to flee from France to Geneva where he had a world-influencing ministry.

G. Campbell Morgan: *The Gospel According to Matthew*. Marshall, Morgan & Scott 1976 Edition. – G. Campbell Morgan (1863-1945) was a renowned preacher, and the Minister of Westminster Chapel, London. In the early half of the 20th century, he drew great crowds to hear his expositions and interpretations of Scripture, which were thought provoking and not always traditional.

Arthur Carr: *The Cambridge Bible for Schools & Colleges, The Gospel According to St. Matthew.* Cambridge University Press 1882. – Arthur Carr (died 1917) was a fellow of Oriel College, Oxford and Assistant Master at Wellington College.

C. H. Dodd: *The Parables of the Kingdom.* Collins, Fontana Books 1961. – Charles Harold Dodd (1884-1973) was Rylands Professor of Biblical Criticism and Exegesis at Manchester University.

William Hendriksen: *New Testament Commentary, The Gospel of Matthew.* The Banner of Truth Trust 1974. – William Hendriksen (1900-1982) was an American ordained minister and New Testament scholar, becoming Professor of New Testament at Calvin Theological Seminary.

G.H. Lang: *Pictures and Parables, Studies in the parabolic teaching of Holy Scripture.* The Paternoster Press, London 1955. – George Henry Lang (1877-1958) was an Open Brethren Bible teacher and author who travelled widely in this country and abroad preaching the gospel.

Harold Lindsell: *Eyre and Spottiswoode Study Bible.* Eyre and Spottiswoode, London, Special Edition. Harold Lindsell (1913-1998) was a respected biblical scholar, author and teacher. He was a founding member of Fuller Theological Seminary and, among many other projects, prepared and edited the introductions, annotations and marginal references to this study Bible.

Martyn Lloyd-Jones: *Studies in the Sermon on the Mount.* Intervarsity Press, Second Edition 1978. – David Martyn Lloyd-Jones (1899-1981) was for thirty years the Minister of Westminster Chapel, London. His expository preaching and writing, undergirded as it was with strong biblical doctrine, has strengthened and encouraged tens of thousands of Christian disciples across the world.

The New Bible Commentary. Edited by Professor F. Davidson, A. M. Stibbs and E.F. Kevan. The Inter-Varsity Fellowship. Second Edition, 1967 reprint.

John Newton: *Jewels from John Newton*, Daily Readings from the Works of John Newton selected by Miller Ferrie. Banner of Truth Trust 2016. – John Newton (1725-1807) was a sea-faring Captain whose heart the Lord totally changed. He became a Church of England Minister at Olney in Buckinghamshire. John Newton was known as 'the letter-writer of the Great Awakening'. He also wrote the hymns *Amazing grace* and *Glorious things of thee are spoken* and a great many others.

J.C.Ryle: *Expository Thoughts on the Gospel, St Matthew*. James Clarke & Co. Ltd. Reprinted 1969. – John Charles Ryle (1816-1900) was for many years Vicar of Stradbroke in Suffolk, where much of his writing took place. He was appointed to be the first Bishop of Liverpool in 1880.

Richard Trench: *Notes on the Parables of Our Lord.* John W. Parker and Son, Eighth Edition, 1860. – Richard Trench (1807-1886) was a biblical scholar whose career included being appointed Dean of Westminster in 1856, and Archbishop of Dublin and all Ireland in 1864.

About the Cover Images, the Author and his Other Publications

The Book Cover
The cover images are from an overland expedition to the Middle East and Jerusalem undertaken by a group of students in 1964. Top row: a country lane near Nazareth; one of us on a borrowed, shepherd's donkey; bottom row: a typical oil lamp; the sea of Galilee – around whose shores and surrounding hills so much of the ministry of Jesus took place.

The Author
(There is a photograph at the foot of the back cover.)
Born in Great Malvern, Worcestershire, England, John Belham has a scientific background, but for most of his life has had the privilege of serving with some very wonderful people, first in suburban ministry, then as Rector of a group of country parishes, and more recently assisting with city ministry. Married with four grown-up children, he delights in the Lord God – his word, his people and his creation.

His spiritual journey
A Praying Teacher, a Crystal Diode and Winter Wheat
A twelve year old lad, headphones on, oblivious to the world, sprawled out at the top of the stairs, right in the way – fiddling with a very simple radio receiver; a crystal set. Will it work? Only if he can get the little wire to touch on the crystal at such a point that it makes a one way electrical gateway; a diode. He tried this way and that, between times adjusting the tuning condenser to search for the different radio stations. Nothing. Then, suddenly, he hit the spot. The little wire,

known as the cat's whisker, was now making contact with a 'sweet spot' and the whole device sprang to life.

A live broadcast filled my headphones and ears. Was it music? Was it the news, the weather or a discussion? No, it was none of these. It was a preacher preaching!

Was it the preaching or the fact that the little, home-built radio set worked? I don't know. But I listened right to the end and, when it finished, determined that I wanted to hear more. The preacher's talks were being relayed by telephone line to a local church, and I asked my Dad to take me to hear him. No razzmatazz, no great build up, nothing visual, just a song and a talk. But through it the Lord God spoke as clearly as any voice, 'John, it is you I want.' I nudged my Dad but he was quite unmoved and, in talking with the minister of the church we attended as a family, he was assured, 'Don't worry, of course he'll soon get over it.' I would have done, but for Miss Gibbs, a teacher at school who taught both English and what was known in those far off days as 'Scripture'. With hindsight, that lady plainly not only taught her youngsters but coveted them for the Lord and prayed for them. It was Miss Gibbs who recognised that the Lord God had begun a work in my life and patiently encouraged me to begin to read the Bible.

The little seed of faith began to grow, springing up like wheat sown in the mild autumn weather. However, as a family, we moved away very soon after that and the next ten years proved to be a very severe spiritual winter, with little or no Christian fellowship or encouragement. Spiritual life withered away, like the wheat in winter; yellowed and to all appearances dead and finished. Until, that is, a spiritual springtime in my twenties saw faith rekindled and the winter-sown wheat vigorously sprouting.

It was the second, tiny 'chance happening' under the hand of God. David, a friend in the local actors' club, offered me a lift.

He was going to a church in 'West Ken', which I took to be a few miles down the road in Kent. It wasn't, it was in Kensington – yet here was the vital Christianity I hadn't encountered since a young schoolboy.

After a while, I was even willing to heed a long-known, nasty, nagging suspicion that the Lord God would have me 'turn my collar round' – to become a Christian minister. It culminated in a prayer that you won't find in any prayer book, 'O.K. Lord, you win.' My employer's reaction astonished me, 'But of course,' as did my landlady's, 'Yes, it is about time you stopped messing about.'

I have had the privilege of marrying, bringing up a family and working for many years among some wonderful people in both city and rural ministry. Day by day I remain thrilled and amazed by the gracious dealing, mercy and love of the Lord God, and just so grateful for his kindness, mercy and patience with such a difficult and wayward son. Yet an adopted son I find myself to be, and one rescued and redeemed by the precious cross of his Son. In the apostle Paul's words, I gladly confess, 'I live by faith in the Son of God who loved me and gave himself for me.' Of course, 'He'll soon get over it.' But, by the grace of the Lord God, I haven't yet, and that was said over sixty years ago!

As you can see, it is the story of God's gracious dealing with a rebellious and unwilling child and could well be summed up as it began – 'saved by a cat's whisker'.

It is in this setting of great thankfulness to my heavenly Father, that the phrases of the Lord's Prayer became such a precious spur to worship and guide and compass for life; so much so that I had to scribble a little book on it to share its jewels with others.

Exploring and Applying the Lord's Prayer
A Prayer to Change the World

Given understanding and a willingness to take it to heart, the Lord's Prayer will not only teach us to pray, it will revolutionise the way we think and the way we live. It is so much more than a gentle murmur. It is a prayer to change the world – beginning with those who pray it.

This is a book highlighting the practical out-working of this greatest of prayers. Chapter by chapter you are invited to explore and apply each phrase, as if you were exploring the rooms of a great mansion. There are questions for personal reflection or discussion.

It is as if you are personally invited to spend time as an honoured guest in a great house. You have complete freedom to enjoy the magnificence of the splendid rooms, but also have freedom to visit the more practical rooms – the kitchens, store rooms, even the bathrooms and security rooms. You are free to meet with members of the household, to admire the furnishings, to pause at the windows and enjoy both the lovely gardens and the fine sweeping views across the estate.

Such, and infinitely greater, is the wonderful invitation given to every disciple within the lines of the Lord's Prayer. Rather than a prayer to be repeated, it is more like a magnificent house to explore.

'Packed with a very great deal of Christian devotion and Biblical teaching . . . with a pastoral touch throughout.'
    Richard Bewes, a former Rector of All Souls Church, Langham Place, London

For further details and to hear the accompanying podcasts visit https://www.lords-prayer.co.uk or search online 'exploring and applying the Lord's Prayer'.

Exploring and Applying the Parables of Jesus
found in the Gospel of Luke

For those with ears to hear, these parables of Jesus speak as sharply and relevantly today as they did 2000 years ago. If you are willing to be stirred and challenged – as the first hearers were – read on. The author invites you to an exploration of each parable in its setting, followed by questions for personal reflection or group discussion.

The book is not intended to be a specialist or academic text but has been written for a wider readership of Christian people. It is currently associated with a website, *exploring and applying the parables*, where podcasts of a number of the parables are offered.

'This is a book to read if you want to gain a deeper understanding of the parables taught by Jesus.'
    Dr. John Clements, Pastor of the Old Meeting House Congregational Church and author of *Strangers and Pilgrims on the Earth*.

www.ingramcontent.com/pod-product-compliance
Lightning Source LLC
Chambersburg PA
CBHW071919290426
44110CB00013B/1417